KT-178-936

The Middle East
A Beginner's Guide

ONEWORLD BEGINNER S GUIDES combine an original, inventive, and engaging approach with expert analysis on subjects ranging from art and history to religion and politics, and everything in between. Innovative and affordable, books in the series are perfect for anyone curious about the way the world works and the big ideas of our time.

Beginners
GUIDES

The Middle East
A Beginner's Guide

Philip Robins

ONEWORLD
OXFORD

A Oneworld Paperback Original

Published by Oneworld Publications 2009

Copyright © Philip Robins 2009

The moral right of Philip Robins to be identified as the Author
of this work has been asserted by him in accordance with
the Copyright, Designs and Patents Act 1988

ISBN 978-1-85168-675-9

Typeset by Jayvee, Trivandrum, India
Cover design by Simon McFadden
Printed and bound in Great Britain by Bell & Bain, Glasgow

Oneworld Publications
185 Banbury Road
Oxford OX2 7AR
England
www.oneworld-publications.com

For my son, Edmund

Contents

Acknowledgements

This book is the distillation of fourteen years teaching Middle East politics and society to undergraduate and Masters students at the University of Oxford. Though this may seem like an improbable cohort with which to develop the parameters of a beginner's guide, in fact at the outset the vast majority of my students were indeed beginners as far as the study of the region is concerned. Yes, they were inquisitive and intelligent beginners, but beginners nevertheless. With very many young people in the West today they share a desire to understand the Middle East, without having had the opportunity to do so before entering higher education. My first words of gratitude must therefore be to the 450 or so graduates of these elective options, who shared their thoughts and their questions and were good enough to listen to my responses.

More broadly, I have been studying, researching and experiencing the Middle East for some thirty-three years. My first visit to the region, to Israel and Palestine, took place in 1976. Since then I have travelled to the region many times, frequently visiting most of its countries, and residing in the region on three occasions. My second word of gratitude must therefore be to the many people of the region, young and old, great and modest, whom I have come into contact with over the years, and who have helped me to develop my ideas about the region. Space precludes even an inadequate attempt to mention some of them by name. I still have much to learn, as do experts and beginners alike. In order to do so there can be no substitute for going to the region and engaging its people in conversation.

Third, I must thank those who have had a special impact upon my career in relation to the Middle East. These include those who have formally taught and substantively assessed my work: the late Nazih Ayubi, David Pool; my doctoral supervisor, Tim Niblock; and Roger Owen. My peers in the current generation of social scientists and modern historians working on the region, with whom I grew up and shared learning and lighter moments: Ali Ansari, Toby Dodge, Mick Dumper, Anoush Ehteshami, Haifaa Jawad, Paul Lalor, Beverly Milton-Edwards, Emma Murphy, Gerd Nonneman, Joel Peters, Richard Schofield, Kirsten Schulze, Claire Spencer and Charles Tripp. And those from the region based in the UK, notably the members of the Holland Park Group, with whom I have had countless debates and discussions over the years, and who have so patiently answered my questions, particularly: Hussein Agha, Mustafa Alani, Hussein Aslan, Saad Djebbar, Jasin Kaplan and Ahmad Khalidi.

I must thank all of my current and past colleagues in Oxford for their congenial company and intellectual stimulation, especially as far as the Middle East is concerned. In particular, I must mention Louise Fawcett, Jim Piscatori (now in sunnier climes) and Michael Willis, and a clutch of thoughtful and dedicated doctoral students, with whom I have shared the task of teaching Middle East Politics over the years. Among colleagues, a special thank you is in order to Ahmed al-Shahi, who read and commented on some of this manuscript. Needless to say the responsibility for the final version of the book is my own.

Lastly, I want to thank the staff of Oneworld for their help and assistance in bringing the idea for a Beginner's Guide on the Middle East to fruition. I must single Mike Harpley out for special thanks. This guide was his idea. He has pursued it, and me, with quiet determination, a constructive attitude and an amiable disposition. Most importantly, he has worked hard to keep both the extravagances of style and substance in check, a contribution for which I am immensely grateful. I must also thank an anonymous reader, for scrutinizing the whole of the first draft and for making a range of helpful comments and suggestions that I have been happy to take on board.

Maps

BLACK SEA
GEORGIA
RUSSIA
ARMENIA
AZERBAIJAN
UZBEKISTAN
TURKEY
AZERBAIJAN
TURKMENISTAN
CASPIAN SEA
CYPRUS
SYRIA
LEBANON
MEDITERRANEAN SEA
IRAQ
ISRAEL
IRAN
AFGANISTAN
GAZA
WEST BANK
JORDAN
KUWAIT
Persian Gulf
PAKISTAN
EGYPT
Gulf of Oman
RED SEA
U A E
SAUDI ARABIA
OMAN
ARABIAN SEA
SUDAN
ERITREA
YEMEN
Gulf of Aden
DJIBOUTI
ETHIOPIA
SOMALIA

Introduction

The Middle East has an image problem. In the minds of most people, in Western countries at least, it is associated with wars, civil strife, revolutionary change, the military in politics, terrorism, human rights abuses, the maltreatment of women, and ethnic and religious minorities. It is often these grotesque and painful images that draw people, from diplomats to journalists to advocacy campaigners, to the region. Even when the images are more potentially positive, such as in the fertile business environment of the oil and gas producing countries of the region, they are rarely soft or benevolent. Making and spending money in the Gulf states is associated with gross excess; consumption is just about as conspicuous as possible.

Such a list prompts one to ask whether it is merely an image problem from which the region suffers or whether it is actually more one of substance? Take two examples. Think wars: there have been five Arab–Israeli conflicts (1948–49, 1956, 1967, 1973, 1982), and there were one million casualties in the 1980–88 war between Iran and Iraq. Consider civil strife: Yemen (1962–67, 1986, 1994); Sudan (1955–72, 1983–2005); Jordan (1970–71); Lebanon (1976–90); Algeria (1992–98); Iraqi Kurdistan (1994–98); Iraq (2003–present) have all experienced bloody civil wars, some intense, some protracted, some both.

As bad as this record of conflict and suffering might be it is important to emphasise from the outset that these experiences are not unique to the region. In other words, the Middle East judged against global standards is not a basket case. Its performance on governance is no worse than was Latin America's up to the 1970s. India and Pakistan have fought three inter-state wars since the 1940s and been on the brink on a number of other occasions. Sub-Saharan Africa's record on civil strife is at least as grave as the Middle East's. Just think of Congo/Zaire. Corruption and clannish politics is similar in practice in the newly independent states of Central Asia.

In some areas the record of the Middle East ranks favourably in comparison with the rest of the globe. Crime rates are well below those experienced in most parts of the world, especially Latin America; Cairo is no Sao Paolo. Family and community solidarity is strong compared with the social atomisation of the advanced capitalist countries. The attitude towards age is especially instructive; in the Middle East there is respect for the experience and wisdom that comes with time, in growing contrast to the impatient and youth-obsessed West.

Placed in such a comparative context the Middle East ranks more closely to other regions, certainly of the developing world. This should not surprise us: the legacy of colonial rule, the recent attempt to build states from unpromising potential, the subsequent shakedown in power and the huge disparities in wealth are all typical of world experience rather than being exceptional to the region.

The next problem to clarify is of what we are speaking when we refer to 'the Middle East'. What is it and where is it? This is a question more easily posed than answered. 'The Middle East' is an elusive term, whether viewed from a geographical, political or ethnic perspective. Unlike most regions of the world – Africa, South America, even southern Asia – the Middle East is not even a geographical expression. Its origins are nineteenth-century colonial; its compass-based reference point betraying the Western European perspective of its inventors. Originally what we now regard as the Middle East would have consisted of North Africa (westwards from Egypt), the Near East (corresponding to the main Arab–Israeli arena), with the Middle East itself more specifically based around the Persian Gulf. Recently, for brevity's sake, it has become common shorthand to collapse all three sub-regions into the expanded catchall of 'the Middle East'.

That gives us a region of about twenty-five countries,* and two major peoples (the Kurds and Palestinians) who have not achieved statehood to match their strongly national consciousness. It runs from Morocco (in Arabic *al-Maghreb* or literally 'place of the west') to Iran; from Turkey in the north to Sudan in the south. This is a space characterised by messy geopolitics. Hence, Sudan straddles the divide between the Middle East and Africa; Turkey operates increasingly in a European as well as a Middle East sphere; Iran looks east as well as west; the North African states are also members of the pan-continental African Union and so on.

Neither does religion nor ethnicity provide coherence. The Middle East is overwhelmingly Muslim, the faith's main holy places (Mecca, Medina, the pilgrimage route, Jerusalem) are to be found there, and Islam is an important part of the identity of the region's inhabitants. But the Middle East does not include Islam's most populous country (Indonesia), nor a majority of its people (only about 430 million out of 1.4 billion globally). While most of the countries of the region are populated predominantly by Arabs (twenty-one states), two of the region's most populous states (Turkey: seventy-five million; Iran: seventy million) are not. The region's strongest military power, Israel, is eighty per cent Jewish. Moreover, many Arab countries have significant minorities, notably Berbers in North Africa, Kurds in Iraq and Syria (as well as Iran and Turkey), and black Africans in southern Sudan; it has been disdain for these inconvenient realities and the homogenising impetus that has often followed that have resulted in intra-country persecutions and even genocide.

A FAVOURITE JOKE

In spite of the anguish and conflict to be found in the region, there is much humour in the Middle East. An old (circa 1989) but characteristic joke goes as follows:

God decides that he has had enough of humanity and will end the world. Being compassionate, he chooses three of the main world leaders, President Bush Senior of the US, President Gorbachev of the USSR and Prime Minister Yitzhak Shamir of Israel, informs them of his decision and allows them two weeks to prepare their peoples for Armageddon. Each in turn addresses their nations. Bush says: 'Fellow Americans, I have some good news and some bad news. The good news is that God exists; the bad that the world will end in a fortnight.' Gorbachev announces: 'Comrades, I have some bad news and some worse news. The first is that God exists, the second is that the world will end soon.' Shamir tells his people: 'Israelis, I have some good news and some great news. The good news is that God exists, the great news is that the Palestinian intifada (uprising) will end in two weeks.'

The joke, which could easily be told against most of the region's leaders, points to the self-preoccupation of the Middle East, where local political issues are often inflated beyond all proportion and where the conceit of monarchs, presidents and prime ministers would lead them to place themselves on a par with the leaders of the world's superpowers.

To recap, the politically incorrect term, 'the Middle East', is used to identify a region that has no geographic or demographic logic to it. It is a region with multiple identities, at the level of the individual, local constituencies and even the state itself. It is afflicted with all of the post-colonial weaknesses and vices that are to be found across the globe. Its building blocks range from the populous (Egypt being the largest Arab state, with seventy-five million people) to the micro (Qatar, with 120,000 nationals). It is a region, not untypical of the world, which socially and politically is not at peace with itself.

If this introduction has begun to point to the fabled complexity, even illogicality, of the Middle East, then it has done its job. Before learning more about the key issues preoccupying the Middle East today, covered in the body of the book, it is first important to know something of the origins of the states and societies of the region, and the extent to which the past conditions the world views of the present. With that in mind the first three chapters will aim to provide a historical background to the contemporary region.

* There are twenty-one member states of the Arab League (plus Palestine), comprising the Arab states of the region. They are further collected into three sub-regional organisations. The six members of the Gulf Cooperation Council are as follows: Bahrain, Kuwait, Oman, Qatar, Saudi Arabia and the United Arab Emirates. The five members of the Arab Maghreb Union are Algeria, Libya, Mauritania, Morocco and Tunisia. The four members of the Arab Cooperation Council, moribund since the Iraqi invasion of Kuwait in August 1990, are Egypt, Iraq, Jordan and Yemen. Other members of the league consist of the Comoros, Djibouti, Lebanon, Somalia, Sudan and Syria. Together with Iran, Israel and Turkey, they comprise the generally acknowledged members of the Middle East.

1

Subjugation

The mutual obsession between the Western world and the East is 2000 years old. It began with Christianity, was fuelled by Islam, was manifest in the Crusades and the Ottoman assault on Europe, and resulted in the humiliating experience of colonialism. It is an intoxicating brew, comprising faith, power and legacy. With the past politicised and often misremembered, there is little prospect of a stable and settled relationship emerging between the West and the Middle East. At best, the two are doomed to mingle and to coexist, with temporary accommodation all that can be hoped for; the alternative is confrontation and intolerance, from which all will suffer.

While this cultural and moral engagement has resulted in prejudices and antipathies on both sides, it is with the Middle East that the view of the other is most vituperative. This is because the last 200 years have been predominantly characterised by the penetration of the East by the West. The decline of the Ottoman Empire compared to its European counterparts suggested the superiority of the West over the East. This became starkly manifest during the era of European colonialism, when most of the societies of the Middle East were subject to an extended period of submission and subjugation. This was a deeply humiliating experience, especially for peoples used to the unchallenged assumption that their religion, Islam (the only permissible 'submission'), was the last and highest form of divine revelation. This experience created a profound crisis of collective self-esteem, from which the Middle East (and indeed much of the Muslim World more generally) has been struggling to come to terms with and recover from ever since.

THE OTTOMAN EMPIRE

The history of the Middle East did not begin with the European entanglement. It was ruled by the Ottoman Empire (the state founded by Othman) for 400 years, until its demise in 1923. Like Europe's great empires of the day, it was vast in size and multi-ethnic in composition. It went further than its European counterparts in being a political organisation in which members of its different ethnic communities could prosper, as long as they pledged their loyalty to the Ottoman state. However, the empire was not entirely equitable in its organisation. Political and social equality only existed among the Muslims of the empire. Christians and Jews (together with Muslims, 'people of the book') were tolerated, and were able to function using their own codes of religious and family law. But they were regarded as second class, and were obliged to pay extra taxes. The empire's internal organisation tended to be loose and decentralised, with local hierarchies co-opted into the imperial structure. The centralisation of the administration grew from the 1830s onwards, the product of a reform strategy (*tanzimat*), as the Ottoman state came more to emulate its European counterparts. This strengthened organisation tended to focus on the main power centres of the empire, like Damascus, its ports and arterial routes. Islam increasingly became the ideological cement of the empire, especially in the late nineteenth century. Attempts at internal democratic reform were quashed by the Sultan of the day in the 1870s. It was only in 1908 that a form of constitutional government was belatedly and briefly adopted.

The modern engagement

The modern engagement between Europe and the Middle East is usually dated from the Napoleonic expedition to Egypt in 1798. This reflected the intellectual and militaristic expansionism of revolutionary France and Western Europe's increasing romance with Egyptology, as the holdings of the British Museum now attest. The French foray was limited in scope and time, in part because of

Admiral Nelson's stunning naval victory on the Nile. It did help trigger a reciprocal relationship, as first Muhammad Ali, the Egyptian leader, and then the Ottoman Empire more generally too sought European ideas as a way to arrest decline, and modernise local administrative and educational practices. The Middle East's borrowings from European modernity were underway.

Attractive though this Napoleonic moment is to commence the modern story, it is somewhat misleading. Trade had been a continuous feature of a cooperative engagement between the Ottoman Empire and the various city states of the European side of the Mediterranean shore since the Middle Ages. European interest in the Persian Gulf had been a result of expanding trade routes to the east. While Holland and Portugal had been the dominant players of the past, it was Britain that emerged as the key force in the Gulf in the last quarter of the eighteenth century. It would remain so for most of the next two hundred years, and represents the first contemporary connection with the region. Most importantly, this relationship was not what we think of when we conjuror up images of colonial exploitation. It was for long periods a relationship based on mutual interest. Though Britain was the stronger party, its involvement on the ground was broadly confined to the strategic heights of policy, certainly during the first century of the relationship. In style and substance, the experience of the British differed radically from much of French colonial practice in the region.

Britain's initial interest in the Gulf was instrumental, an aspect of its colonial 'jewel in the crown', India. The Persian Gulf waterway was at that time beset by piracy, as was much of the region (this being the era of the infamous Barbary piracy off North Africa). In order to protect its trade routes to India, Britain needed to address the precarious security of the Gulf waterway. It did so not through the use of military means, but through diplomacy. It negotiated and concluded a series of agreements in 1820, 1835 and 1852 with the rulers of the statelets of the Arabian side of the Gulf, whereby the local ruling families agreed to cooperate in the eradication of piracy in return for two things: the payment of a financial subsidy, and political recognition. Given that these local leaders had hitherto been 'taxing' the activity of the local pirates, it was both a successful and a reciprocal piece of negotiation. Its outcome would render the Gulf safe for commercial shipping for the next two centuries.

In their substance, these agreements were arguably of even more benefit to the local leaders. The British subsidies guaranteed them an income in perpetuity. Given the small size of these entities, and the undeveloped nature of the local economies, these subsidies were large enough to be distributed as patronage, in exchange for the political loyalty of their subjects. They also ensured that the local leaders might despatch their leadership roles in keeping with the cultural standards of the day: for example, through the dispensing of hospitality, and generosity more generally. More importantly, the recognition of the local leaderships by the British had the effect of cementing these local families in positions of power, again in perpetuity. Rather than a dynamic process of clans and tribes from the desert interior challenging and displacing the family leaderships of these coastal statelets, as had been the experience hitherto, the effect of the British involvement was to fossilise the traditional political hierarchies of the littoral. It is notable that the ruling families of today – the al-Sabah in Kuwait, the Khalifa in Bahrain and the al-Thani in Qatar – all held sway when British pragmatism was applied to what would subsequently become officially known as 'the Trucial Coast', a zone of peace.

Classical colonialism

If Britain's two centuries' involvement in the Gulf was light, reciprocal and resulted in a legacy of stability and continuity, this was generally untypical of the colonial experiences of the rest of the region. At the other end of the continuum of colonial experience was that of the French in Algeria. This involvement would also be long, but would be altogether much more penetrative and one-sided than in the Gulf. With their avowed goal to 'civilise the natives' (*mission civilatrice*), France would at different times attempt nothing less than the transformation of the economy, politics, culture and even the religion of the country, in favour of complete Francification. That the project was far from being a failure can be seen in the prominence of the French language in Algeria today, and the thriving commercial, educational and demographic relations between Algeria and metropolitan France. That it is by no means a happy legacy can be seen in the *kulturkampf* (literally 'culture struggle') that divides contemporary Algeria, with the Francophone elite, or 'parti du France', as it is disparagingly referred to, enjoying political power and economic wealth. Those Algerians identifying themselves as Arab and Muslim, the vast majority of the population, have been economically and politically peripheralised.[*]

Even in Algeria, the original involvement of the French was far from cynically exploitative, at least in its origins. The first foray into North Africa in 1830 owed more to domestic political dynamics in France, as the bourgeois monarchy of Louis-Phillippe stuttered to an end, than to an orchestrated exercise in external domination. Once the French presence had been established in Algeria, and the backdrop of the age of empires in Europe had begun to emerge, Paris embraced its mission with gusto. A large settler community, the *pied noir* (lit. 'black foot'), some one million strong at its zenith, formed the core of the French presence in Algeria.

France's colonial interest in the nineteenth century was eventually widened to take in the adjacent North African territories of Morocco and Tunisia. France's cultural mission was extended to those entities as well, with French still widely spoken in both countries today. The Eucharistic Congress, a celebration of French Catholicism in Tunisia in 1930, for example, shows both the self-confidence of the French colonial establishment, and its imprudent disdain for tenacious local religious values. Even so, Morocco and Tunisia never experienced the thorough-going nature of French rule that was witnessed in Algeria. In the former, local political hierarchies were retained, and the monarchy, after a brief period of suppression in the early 1950s, still holds sway in Morocco today. Algeria, by contrast, was not regarded as a colonial possession; rather it was integrated into the very structure of government of metropolitan France. Algerian representatives even sat in the French parliament, though to acquire French citizenship Muslim Algerians were obliged to renounce their faith.

Though the Algerian case was an extreme one in its transform-atory ambition, it provided the template for the Italian colonial venture in Libya, and to a certain extent the British experiences in Egypt. The Italian adventure in Libya began in 1911 and hence predated Fascism. It was marked by great initial frustration, as, apart from a handful of small towns, Libya consisted of a large expanse of desert, populated by nomadic tribes. Italy's conventional army struggled to subdue these sparsely populated areas, where the speed of movement of the mounted Bedouin tribes and their knowledge of local terrain, together with the network of lodges of the local religious leaders, the Sanussiyah, drove the Italians to increasing degrees of frustration. The colonial response was to be ever more draconian. Eventually the opponents of Italian rule were subdued through the establishment of enclosed areas, akin to concentration camps in the desert. The swashbuckling leader of the resistance, Omar Mukhtar (played by Anthony Quinn in the film *Lion of the Desert*, 1981), was eventually caught and hanged. Large numbers of Italian settlers went to Libya to administer the new territory, to trade and to farm. Italian colonial possessions were then extended under the Fascists to cover Italian

Somaliland and Abyssinia (Ethiopia). These would remain under their control until the defeat of the Axis powers in the Second World War.

Britain's initial involvement in Egypt in the nineteenth century was reminiscent of its arrival in the Gulf or indeed in India, in that the economic aspect of the engagement drove the strategic, rather than high politics. In this case, it was the desire to build the Suez Canal, a joint Anglo-French inspired and owned engineering wonder, which provided the bridgehead. The impetus for the project was again India, with Britain keen to cut down the journey time (not to mention the more precarious nature of the route) via the Cape of Good Hope. The presence of the Suez Canal would dominate British strategic thinking in the Middle East for a century to come.

The project brought many British engineers and financiers to Egypt, and their business interests inevitably widened with their engagement with the state of Muhammad Ali's successors, the Khedives. The poor financial control of the ailing Egyptian state, egged on by these new market-makers, saw the regime become increasingly profligate and dependent. A financial crisis and credit crunch inevitably ensued. This final financial default was accompanied by politically inspired anti-British protests. They resulted in Britain stepping in to take over responsibility for the key areas of government of the country in 1882.

The period between 1883 and 1907 would be dominated by one of the big British figures of empire of the day, Sir Evelyn Baring, later to become Lord Cromer. With his patrician haughtiness and his air of cultural supremacy, Cromer was doubly prejudiced against the local population. For Egypt, this was difficult to bear. It was the largest and most strategically important of the Arab countries, itself having been a dynamic and expansionist state under Muhammad Ali, just two generations before. It was also host to the highest seat of Islamic learning at al-Azhar University (founded in 969) in Cairo. The depth of Egyptian

resentment against Cromer and the imperial system of government would remain a raw one, as evidenced as late as the 1950s,
and the Suez Crisis. In the meantime, Egypt would remain
totally subjugated until 1916, and the formal ending of the
protectorate in order to garner political support for the British
war effort. In 1922 Egypt was granted a nominal independence,
as Britain sought to repackage empire.

The mandate system

While countries like Britain, France, Italy and to a lesser extent
Spain made selected, colonial inroads into the territories of the
Middle East during the nineteenth and early twentieth centuries,
the Ottoman Empire (see box on p. 2) remained the accepted if
nominal government across the remainder of the region until
the First World War. The Ottomans' disastrous miscalculation in
backing Germany and Austro-Hungary in the Great War
resulted in it sharing in the defeat of 1918. With the US's retreat
into isolationism, Britain and France were left as the regionally
dominant great powers of the day. As with the old imperial state
of Austria, the Ottomans' multi-national empire was dismantled.

During the First World War, Britain and France had toyed
with various visions of the future of the Middle East. Their ideas
were driven by the needs of fighting the war. Hence, Britain had
entered into a loose understanding with the Sherif Hussein of
Mecca (the Hussein-McMahon correspondence) in order to try
to foment disunity behind Ottoman lines. Sherif Hussein was a
Hashemite (see box opposite), and as such claimed lineage back
to the Prophet Muhammad, thereby giving him some religious
authority and prestige on the ground. He agreed to enter the
war in alliance with Britain in the belief that victory would
result in his inheriting a large part of the Ottoman territories
roughly corresponding to the Levant and northern Arabia. The

Hashemite alliance was useful for Britain, as it refuted Ottoman attempts to portray the war in strictly religious terms as the 'clash of civilisations' of its day. It also enabled the British to open a second front in the Red Sea area, immortalised in the guerrilla

THE HASHEMITES

The Hashemites claim to be able to trace their genealogy back to the House of Hashem, the clan of the Prophet Muhammad. Their religious legitimacy was further entrenched by the fact that successive Ottoman sultans looked to them to administer the holy city of Mecca. As the empire unravelled, the Hashemites used this platform to expand their authority. This resulted in a bid for regional power during the First World War, dynastic ambition being hidden behind an ideological cloak of an early wave of Arab nationalism. Through the Hussein-McMahon correspondence of 1915–16, Sharif Hussein of Mecca believed that he had a British commitment to the establishment of an independent Arab successor state under his leadership. On this basis, he declared war on the Ottomans in 1916. In reality, the dynamics of great power politics proved to have more traction than relations with regional leaders, and Britain had little choice but to agree to French mandatory control of Syria and Lebanon. However, the small group of influential British Arabist advisors at the Versailles peace conference, like T.E.Lawrence and Gertrude Bell, felt a strong political debt to the Hashemites. Consequently, once displaced by the French from Damascus, Sharif Hussein's son, Faisal, was established on a newly created throne in Iraq under overall British supervision. A second son, Abdullah, was later recognised as the ruler of another new state, Jordan. Hashemites would reign in Baghdad until an army takeover in 1958; they remain in power in Amman. Sharif Hussein was less fortunate. He died in exile in 1931, having lost his power base of the Kingdom of the Hijaz, based on Mecca, to the emerging Saudi state of the Arabian interior. Embittered by his treatment, Sharif Hussein had spurned a continuing relationship with the British, thereby leaving his kingdom weakened and open to attack.

warfare of T.E.Lawrence and Sherif Hussein's son, Amir Faisal, (played by Peter O'Toole and Alec Guinness respectively in the famous David Lean movie, *Lawrence of Arabia*).

On 2 November 1917 the British government released the Balfour Declaration, in an attempt to win over Jewish opinion in central Europe and North America. The brief statement said that London looked favourably on the establishment of 'a national home' (as opposed to a state) in Palestine for the Jewish people, as long as it was established without prejudice to the 'civil and religious rights of existing non-Jewish communities' (overwhelmingly the Arab residents). The Balfour Declaration did not contradict the apparent undertaking to Sherif Hussein, but it did muddy the water, and created the circumstances for rival state-building projects in Palestine between the 1920s and the 1940s. Lastly, Britain and France entered into a secret bilateral negotiation (Sykes-Picot Agreement, after the respective diplomats that conducted it) about what to do with the former Ottoman territories at the end of the war. Here, the logic of great power interests trumped the regional bargains, and fostered an enduring sense of Arab grievance that remains today. According to Sykes-Picot, London and Paris agreed to carve up the Levant and Mesopotamia to their own advantage. The blueprint of the colonial configuration of the next two decades had been laid down.

The collapse of the Ottoman Empire left Britain and France in day to day control on the ground. As ever, possession was to prove to be nine-tenths of ownership. The Paris peace conference set about the establishment of a new, post-war, world order. The atmosphere that prevailed was post-imperial, in that the naked seizure of territory and the control of associated peoples was no longer regarded as being morally acceptable. The US president, Woodrow Wilson, wished to see the principle of self-determination prevail in the creation of this order. But US influence waned dramatically after Congress chose to recommit itself to the Monroe Doctrine and turn its back on the world beyond its own hemisphere. The Middle East subsequently became subject to a compromise. In the name of delicacy, the European colonial powers would be discreet about their imperial intentions, hiding them behind a paternalistic commitment to the preparation of societies on the ground for political independence. The mandate system, to be operated by the newly established League of Nations, was duly born at the conference of San Remo in Italy in April 1920.

Britain was to be the mandatory power for Palestine, Transjordan (since 1946, the Hashemite Kingdom of Jordan) and Iraq, a reflection of its preoccupation with lateral strategic considerations, with India ultimately in mind. France was to be the responsible power for Syria and an enlarged Lebanon, where, through the Maronite Roman Catholic community, it had exerted increasing interference during the later stages of the Ottoman Empire. In order to establish itself on the ground the French first had to displace a somewhat chaotic Arab government, based in Damascus, which had already declared the Hashemite Amir Faisal to be king. The outcome was only confirmed once the French had defeated an Arab army at Maysalun in July 1920.

The period between 1918 and 1923 was the genesis of the region's statehood, its story of creation. It was key as far as the making of the modern Middle East is concerned. It represented a period of transition whereby the Middle East was transformed from an Ottoman core, with European encroachments at the edges, to becoming virtually an extension of the European empires that now reached around much of the world. The speed and profundity of the change, and the collapse of the world's leading Muslim state, etched this into a period of trauma and dishonour for most of the region.

This period was vital in the creation of the contemporary Middle East state system. The boundaries that were drawn and the entities that were created would largely define the states that would emerge. It is these states, virtually without amendment let alone change, which, in all of their idiosyncracies and imperfections, continue to exist today. For all of their multiple and apparently contradictory promises of the First World War, the outcome, though noisy and difficult in places, was on the whole reasonably smooth. Britain and France did divide the Levant according to Sykes-Picot. Sherif Hussein may not have ruled over a single dynastic state, but Hashemites did preside over Iraq and Transjordan, as well as ruling the Hijaz (admittedly only briefly) from Mecca, the seat of Islam. Only in Palestine would wartime promises, alluringly even-handed though they might have seemed at the time, prove to be incompatible with the new responsibilities on the ground. The Balfour Declaration may have been an elegant exercise in drafting, but its name is still cursed on the Arab street today.

BA'THISM

Ba'thism was an ideological movement of Arab nationalism with strong fascist overtones, which emerged among Arab intellectuals who had studied in Europe in the early twentieth century. Michel Aflaq and Salah ad-Din Bitar are usually acknowledged as its founding fathers. Though hazy in its detail, Ba'thism latched onto the slogans of '[Arab political] unity, freedom [from colonial subjugation] and socialism'. The word 'ba'th', meaning resurrection, points to the utopian nature of its ideas. Despite its highbrow origins, Ba'thist movements became a magnet for ambitious political outsiders in the region: the Alawi minority in Syria; rural Shia and Sunnis in Iraq; Christians in Jordan. Ba'thism was catapulted into an ideology of state power with military coups in its name in Syria in 1963 and Iraq in July 1968. Its cult of violence, allied with the peasant background of much of its elite membership, meant that Ba'thism became identified with the authoritarian practice of politics. In reality, political doctrine came increasingly to serve the interests of its respective leadership, Saddam Hussein in Iraq and Hafez al-Asad in Syria. Ba'thism collapsed in Iraq after thirty-five years as the movement of power with the US-led invasion of 2003. It remains, nominally at least, the ideology of the prevailing regime in Syria.

Though it grew steadily, Arab nationalism was still a minority interest on the margins of the politics of the region into the 1940s. What catapulted the ideology to real prominence was the wave of regime changes that swept the Middle East in the late 1940s and 1950s, led, as the CUP had been, by a cluster of middle ranking military officers. In search of a belief system to explain their political dissatisfaction, and sensitive that their seizure of power might be regarded as entirely self-serving, these officers latched onto Arab nationalism, which provided both a critique of European colonialism and its local allies, and a pathway towards mass mobilisation, cross-regional solidarity and

2
Resistance

In the Middle East, the onset of colonialism eventually precipitated a backlash. Thus was born a struggle that would last until the end of the last vestiges of colonial rule. The pattern is not that dissimilar to the broad experiences of the developing world, and Sub-Saharan Africa in particular. At first this resistance was based on local solidarities, such as clan, village and province. Increasingly, national collective feeling came to give coherence and broader appeal. And religion was never far away from the nationalist-based resistance that emerged, giving it a wider and deeper resonance. For Islam viewed the European colonialism as both unjust and alien. It gave moral authority to the resistance of such projects, including where violence was used as an instrument of this resistance.

The new nationalisms

The Ottoman Empire was a multi-ethnic, multi-cultural organisation for which the Islamic religion was, especially towards the end, its ideological cement. Compared with the mainstream European experience, a sense of ethno-nationalism was slow to emerge. Conceptually, Islam and nationalism were at opposite poles of attraction: if religion created solidarities between Turks and Kurds and Arabs, then what is the need for particularistic nationalisms which would only create separate identities and hence divide them? This proved to be a sustainable approach until the last quarter of the nineteenth century, and the growth of the Young Turk movement. The latest movement to embark upon the perennial quest of why the empire was in decline, the Young Turks concluded it was because the Ottomans had not absorbed the ideas and identity of Europe's ideology of the moment, ethno-nationalism. The emphasis placed on Turkish nationalism was also a convenience in terms of internal Ottoman politics, as it helped to differentiate the Young Turks from the autocratic Sultan, Abdul Hamid II, who was associated with the idea that Islam was the empire's ideological glue. Thus was begun a movement to this end.

The rise of Turkish nationalism was swift. This was not because it was a mass based ideology; rather it was associated with a small number of urban centres of the empire, and with the rising elites, especially army officers. The reason for the prominence of Turkish nationalism was its propagation by the Committee on Union and Progress (CUP), an underground movement which seized power in 1908 and deposed Abdul Hamid, rendering his handful of brief successors only nominal heads of state. Turkish nationalism had risen to prominence because it had suddenly become the ideology of the state, and hence could rely upon the instruments of the state for its dissemination and propagation.

Faced with the surge in importance of Turkish nationalism, and with the Islamic solidarity movement discredited and on the decline, it was only a matter of time before other aspirant national groups in the empire began to apply the ideas of European ethno-nationalism to their own predicament. For the large Arab component of the empire this began around the turn of the century, through a handful of intellectuals. For other groups, such as the Kurds, with their intensely tribalised social setting, ethno-nationalism would be confined to a couple of urban centres, such as Diyarbakir in south-eastern Turkey and Suleimaniya in northern Iraq, until well after the Second World War.

The new nascent nationalisms of the Ottoman Empire's

periphery received a boost with the adoption of constitu[…] ism by the CUP. This included the creation of a parliam[…] focal point for the different peoples of the empire, th[…] drawing attention to the cultural diversity of the entity. Bec[…] of their demographic size, Arab representation was visible wi[…] the new institutions of the state. However, nationalism was s[…] to take root: Arab representation was in great part a patric[…] affair. This was, after-all, as the late twentieth-century doyen[…] Arab commentators, Albert Hourani, has described it, 'the era[…] notable politics'. When in 1916 the Hashemites raised th[…] standard of the so-called 'Great Arab Revolt', in league with th[…] British and against the Ottomans, it was at least as likely to be[…] viewed in terms of dynastic ambition as Arab nationalist solidarity. During the First World War the vast majority of Muslims in[…] the empire, Arabs included, rallied behind the Ottoman banner of Islamic solidarity against the infidels.

Arab nationalist ideas continued to circulate and grow after the Versailles peace settlement in the aftermath of the First World War, but from a low base. They were mostly confined to the intellectual and cultural centres of the Arab world, notably Damascus and Beirut. They were reliant for circulation upon a small but dedicated group of intellectuals, the leaders of whom had been educated in Europe, often in Paris. One such figure was Michel Aflaq, who would acquire fame as a co-founder of the Ba'th Party. The ideas of nationalism were especially attractive to Arab Christians, because they provided space for Christian activism in radical, anti-European politics, without the difficulties of those ideas being too closely associated with Islam. It was also a strategy of self-preservation: if Christians were openly opposed to the Imperialism of the Christian world they were less vulnerable to accusations of collaboration, and the retributive violence that could follow. It was in the high schools and universities of the Arab world that these ideas would circulate.

renewed political glory. Like Turkish nationalism, Arab nationalism had suddenly shot to stardom as a state patronised ideology. In doing so, it would acquire a mass following but would
lose its soul.

Turkish war of independence

In view of the timelines of the emergence of the new nationalisms of the Orient, it should not be a surprise which became
the first and most efficient of vehicles for resisting European
colonial encroachment. There can be no doubt that the most
effective indeed breathtaking example of resistance to the
European colonial vision for the Middle East came with the
Turkish war of independence. It was a demonstration of what
could be achieved by a subjugated people, even at what
appeared to be the height of European superpower hegemony.
Moreover, it was achieved in a context of military defeat, state
collapse, widespread poverty, massive refugee in-flows and
collective national humiliation. Though now forgotten in
outline let alone detail by all except for the Turks themselves, it
stands as one of the great demonstrations of collective national
will in the modern age. However, rather than emerging as a
template for resistance in the Middle East of its day, it ended up
proving to be a heroic anachronism; a major exception to the
regional rule of acquiescence, at least until the Algerian struggle
for independence more than three decades later.

In 1918 the game was up for the Ottoman Empire. With
Istanbul occupied by British and French forces and with the
Sultan a tool in European hands, any form of resistance seemed
futile and improbable. This post-war power configuration was
given a formal political shape by the 1920 Treaty of Sevres,
which provided for the disposal of the former Ottoman territories. If the Middle East provinces had already gone, Sevres

sought to divide up the lands closest to home. Anatolia, then widely known as 'Asia Minor', was to be divided into zones of French, Greek and Italian control. The Armenians, who had suffered so grievously during the First World War, had the chance for a state of their own. There was even a perspective on Kurdish political independence. The Turks themselves were to be left with a modest area of land in the impoverished Anatolian interior.

In 1920 Greek armies landed in order to implement Sevres. It seemed that their success was inevitable. But this was to be no updated version of *The Iliad*. The first stirring of Turkish resistance had shown itself in 1918, with the galvanising of a national movement and the adoption of an associated manifesto, the National Pact. This document sought to define those areas in which Turks were a majority and which should properly be included in a Turkish nation-state. Eschewing an Ottoman-style desire to reconquer lost territories in the Middle East, the Pact focused on the incorporation of Anatolia and some adjacent territories into a Turkish state. In its vision the drafters of the Pact built upon the Young Turk movement of the late nineteenth/early twentieth centuries, which had first elaborated a nationally self-conscious Turkish (as opposed to multi-ethnic Ottoman) approach to political identity.

With a vision and a collective national sense, what the Turkish nationalists required was leadership and generalship. They found that in Mustafa Kemal (aka Ataturk, the 'father of the Turks'), a war hero from the defence of Gallipoli during the First World War, and a band of officers who had rallied to his standard in central Anatolia, far from the humiliations of Istanbul. A desperate military campaign then ensued, with the French army in the south-east of the country contained and subdued. With both Britain and France suffering from acute post-war over-stretch, neither was willing to draw out the campaign, especially with the Turkish nationalists resisting so stoutly. The Greek armies, meanwhile, had been repeatedly defeated in the west of the country. They were driven away and Smyrna (now Izmir), with its large Greek population, was torched.

Flush with its decisive military campaign, the nationalists pressed their advantage diplomatically. Unworkable, Sevres was put aside. A new treaty was signed at Lausanne in 1923, at which the international community simply recognised the outcome of the war. The foreign zones of influence idea was abandoned. Greek and Turkish population exchanges consolidated the ethnic separation upon which the notion of a Turkish nation-state was presupposed. All ideas of Armenian, let alone Kurdish, self-determination were no longer practicable. The occupation of Istanbul was lifted, though to consolidate the strategic depth of the new state the small interior town of Ankara was confirmed as the new capital. Most of the lands defined by the National Pact were incorporated into the newly created Republic of Turkey. The one exception was the old Ottoman province of Mosul, which Britain insisted on including in its mandate for Iraq. The new authorities in Ankara had no choice in the matter, but pragmatically accepted the outcome in exchange for the international legitimacy of League of Nations membership. The Turkish nationalists had bought the necessary time to impose their vision of a Turkish nation-state on those other population groups in Anatolia for which Turkishness was not the most salient national identity.

Other independent spaces

If the Turkish case was the most breathtaking example of a successful resistance to the Europeans, it was not the only space in the region to be free of imperialism. Neither Saudi Arabia nor Iran fell directly under the extended control of the European imperial powers. The Saudi case is the most eye-catching. For while Britain was adding to its portfolio of colonial lands, the emerging Saudi state was doing exactly the same thing in central Arabia during the first three decades of the twentieth century. The emergence of modern Saudi Arabia is as much a story of conquest and subjugation as any in the region at the time.

Britain already had control of the Gulf emirates by the end of the nineteenth century. It then extended its area of control through the acquisition of the mandates of Iraq, Transjordan and Palestine in the early 1920s. However, a vast area of land, much of it arid and ecologically marginal, lay at the centre of Britain's quadrilateral of control. This area, with its scattered dusty towns, its difficult trade routes and marginal agriculture, had seen political control fluctuate for centuries, as individual clans fleetingly held sway. There had already been two chieftancies of the Saud clan, states in the making, which had subsequently dissolved in an endless dynamic of internal disunity and rival clan challenge.

Given the timeline of colonialism it is probably just as well that Abdul Aziz bin Saud began the reassertion of Saudi power in the first months of the twentieth century, through the takeover of Riyadh. Over the next two decades, the resurgent Saud would conquer and incorporate four regions of Arabia: from the Najd in the geographical centre, based on Riyadh; to Hasa, the eastern province; the Asir, lying adjacent to Yemen in the south-west; and then the Hijaz, the former seat of the Hashemites, with its focal point of the holiest places of the Islamic faith, in the north-west. The secret of the success of this rapid run of victories was the mixing of Bedouin values of corporate solidarity ('*asabiyah)* and warlike posturing, with the puritanical intolerance of the Unitarian or Wahhabi sect of Islam. If the Bedouin brought the admiration for warlike prowess to the mix, the Wahhabi religious sheikhs brought an unshakeable sense of righteousness, allied with a disdain for the less godly.

WAHHABISM

Wahhabism, a variant of Sunni Islam, originated in the eighteenth century in what is today Saudi Arabia. Wahhabism refers to the teachings of its founder, Muhammad ibn Abdul Wahhab, which advocate a puritanical return to the real or imagined basics of the religion. These include: emulating the rituals and values of the heyday of Islam; disdain for the Shia and other heterodox 'Muslims'; antipathy towards non-Muslims; and strict gender segregation. At the time of its emergence Wahhabism formed an alliance with the temporal rulers of the day, the Al Saud. Though the fortunes of the Saudis have waxed and waned, the alliance has remained in place. Wahhabi Islam is the dominant religious movement in Saudi Arabia today. The descendants of the founder, the al-Sheikh family, have inter-married with the Al Saud, and are regularly given ministries in the cabinet, especially those, like justice, which help to renew the values of Wahhabism in the country. Wahhabi ideas have inspired the likes of Osama bin Laden and al-Qaida, as well as the conserva- tive teachers (*ulema*), who fill the majority of the posts in the religious hierarchy in the kingdom. Considerable funds are channelled through Saudi religious foundations to spread the goals and values of Wahhabi Islam across the Islamic and non-Islamic world, including Europe and North America.

The rapid success for the sword of Wahhabi Islam soon came to threaten adjacent British interests. Abdul Aziz faced a dilemma: accommodate the British or gamble all on God's support for a new wave of religious expansionism. He pragmat- ically chose the former, purging the tribal shock troops (*Ikhwan* or brotherhood) in the late 1920s, when they differed in outlook. The Saud-Wahhabi alliance remained central to the nature of power in Saudi Arabia, with temporal and religious authority respectively allied together.

If the Saudi–British relationship was one of mutual contain- ment and parallel political consolidation, the Anglo-Iranian interaction was much more multi-pronged and controversial. Though Britain never came actually to subjugate Iran, its actions were hardly benign. They can best be divided into three phases. First came the period of economic colonialism, when Britain succeeded in imposing commercial agreements on Iran which were advantageous to itself but deeply disadvantageous to local Iranian interests. The most obvious example of this was the tobacco monopoly, concluded in the 1890s, when the old Qajar dynasty (the Ottoman equivalent in Iran) was enfeebled and in terminal decline. Britain's avaricious interests in Iran's primary goods sector would soon after extend to Iranian oil, discovered in 1908, and the mainstay of the world's new oil-based economy for the first three decades of its existence.

The second painful engagement between Iran and the forces of European imperialism came during the Second World War, following two decades of rule by Reza Shah, the army officer who had seized power in 1921 and set up the fleeting Pahlavi dynasty. Reza Shah had established a widespread programme of social reform in the 1920s and 1930s, resonant of Ataturk's modernist impact in Turkey. However, by the 1940s he was dabbling in international politics and out of his depth. Britain and the USSR consequently occupied Iran, in southern and northern zones respectively, to ensure its enforced support during wartime, and Reza Shah was removed. The occupation ended in the mid-1940s. But only after the Soviet Union had, in a forerunner of the Cold War, dragged its heels on withdrawal, leaving behind fragile, separate Azarbaijani and Kurdish entities, soon to collapse. For Iranians, their independence appeared to be under sustained attack, with their ethnic minorities a potential fifth column for outside powers.

The third difficult engagement with colonialism came over oil in the early 1950s, following the Pahlavi restoration. Mohammed Mossadeq, a recently elected nationalist reformer, had nationalised the Anglo-Iranian Oil Company (AIOC), the forerunner to BP, an early example of the resource nationalism that would sweep the Third World two decades later. Britain enlisted the US in the form of the CIA, in a piece of classic skulduggery, financing mob violence to weaken Mossadeq and bring about his eventual downfall. Ever since, Iranians have had an exaggerated respect for the depths of Britain's deviousness. With the conspiracy a success, Reza Shah's son, Mohammed, was re-established in Tehran, soon to entrench himself as an autocrat, and the ownership of the AIOC secured. It is now popular for historians of the region, in an exercise in counter-factuals, to lament that if the Shah had not been restored in such a way the polarisation that formed the backdrop to the events of the 1978–79 Iranian revolution would not have existed and hence the revolution would not have taken place.

Arab resistance

Other attempts at defying the colonial tide were rather less successful. The best known cases of Arab resistance are the Urabi Revolt in Egypt, arguably the first of its kind, the Iraqi 'revolution' of 1920 and the 1936–39 Arab revolt in Palestine. All ended in failure, but all provided a powerful story that still resonates and inspires today.

The first piece of resistance to the forces of European colonialism to acquire the status of legend was the Urabi Revolt in Egypt, 1879–82. The revolt took place just after the displacement of the ruler, Khedive Ismail, who had been responsible for Egypt's deep indebtedness, by his son, Tewfiq, a more compliant figure, with British connivance. It was led by Colonel Ahmad Urabi, a career soldier of peasant stock, who had worked himself up through the ranks to head the Egyptian army. He opposed the role of foreign elites in the running of the country, especially after Tewfiq had drastically cut the size of the army as a cost cutting measure. This focus of national disaffection was bolstered by the Egyptian peasantry, who bridled under the multiple burdens of taxation, public works gangs and unregulated foreign involvement. Urabi threw down the gauntlet, and Egypt was divided in two, very much along class lines.

Of course Urabi and his supporters had little chance of success as long as Britain was willing to commit the necessary military resources to the restoration of its control, which it was. With the alliance between the British, the large landowners, the wealthy Syrian merchants and the upper stratum of officials a solid one, Urabi's time was finite. He was defeated by a British force at Tel el-Kebir, and lived the rest of his life in exile in Ceylon. However, the importance of Urabi was more in what he represented than what he accomplished. He had stood up to the British and their local supporters, and had, at least temporarily, held his own. The symbolism of an independent-spirited effort, aimed at addressing the interests of the vast majority of Egyptians, had potent symbolic meaning. Moreover, the fact that his support would be articulated in terms of 'Egypt for the Egyptians', Copt and Muslim alike, was an important demonstration of the collective national identity that prevailed on the ground. Finally, Urabi had set the template for another colonel who would enjoy rather greater political success against the British in some eighty years time, Colonel Gamal Abdul Nasser.

The story of the Iraq revolt of 1920 has recently gained a new lease of life because of the 2003 Iraq war for regime change, and its aftermath of anti-American resistance and civil violence. Today, the 1920 revolt is celebrated by Iraqi nationalists as a united Iraqi effort to prevent the establishment of the British mandate. The reality was that widespread misgivings about the emerging order translated into a revolt against the new authority of the British by the overwhelmingly Shia tribes of the central Euphrates. The revolt was spirited and Britain struggled over a number of months to contain and suppress it. At around

500, significant numbers of British troops were killed. Iraqi fatalities ran at twelve times that number. The origin of the uprising had less to do with Iraqi nationalism, however. It was an amalgam of issues, encompassing religious and resource factors and the power and wealth that were associated with these, rather than the more abstract notions of ideology and identity.

In its own immediate way the revolt was not totally unsuccessful. It brought home to the somewhat complacent British authorities the cost of the occupation and subjugation of a country the size of Iraq, especially with its background of grievance. Britain's decision to grant Iraq increased autonomy in 1922 and nominal independence in 1932 was born of its experiences in 1920. London's sub-contracting of Iraqi governance to the Faisali branch of the Hashemites reflected a wish not to become directly embroiled in the governance of a fractious country. Ultimately and ironically it was the Shia Arabs of Iraq that lost most from the 1920 revolt. While its members did the fighting, Arab Sunni elites of the day connived with the British to maintain the administration of the country in their hands, as it had been during the Ottoman centuries. It would take another eighty years of in part a double subjugation (British and Sunni Arab) before the Shia of Iraq would exercise a degree of national political authority justified by their demographic majority.

Doomed resistance also characterised a crucial phase of Arab experience in the British mandate of Palestine. Here, resistance was not so much focused on the British presence itself, but on the policies implemented by Britain as the political authority in relation to Jewish immigration. Initially, the inflow of Jewish migrants had not been a problem in Palestine: their numbers were relatively small and they helped stimulate the local economy. As the 'push' factor of European anti-semitism increased their numbers, British partiality on the migration question and the vigorous activism of Zionist bodies, notably the land purchases of the Jewish Agency, alienated the local Arab communities. The displacement of Arab tenant farmers, follow-ing land sales by Arab absentee landlords, bred increasing levels of local disquiet. This resulted in the first major display of violent Arab opposition, with the Wailing Wall protests of 1929.

Thereafter the political context of Jewish immigration remained highly charged and politicised. This spilt over into revolt and civil resistance in 1936, marking the beginning of a three year period of active resistance to mandate policy. Hindsight would show that the nature and timing of the revolt was disastrous for the Arab side. The long, drawn-out struggle impoverished the Arab economy in Palestine, without degrading the capacity of the nascent Jewish state, which functioned independent of Arab society and its economy. Britain's seizures of arms caches and the eventual arrest or death of its leaders emasculated the Arab side for a generation, just as the Hagannah (Jewish defence force) was busy increasing its capacity, having foreseen what would become the independence war of 1948–49. London did enact a review of its immigration policy in response to the revolt, and subsequently adopted a policy which was more even-handed. By that stage, however, time was fast running out for the British presence in Palestine, thereby giving any even-handed policy made in London a short shelf life. Moreover, the Second World War was now being fought; future revelations of the Nazis' Final Solution would render British attempts to limit Jewish immigration morally and practically untenable.

Like Urabi, and Iraq in 1920, the Arab revolt in Palestine was more important as a model and as an example than in the results achieved at the time. The Arab revolt was to resonate with the first and second Palestinian *intifada* (uprisings) of 1987–93 and 2000 onwards. For example, Izzedin al Qassam, one of the military leaders killed in the 1936–39 revolt, was to live on in the name of the Hamas' military wing, the Izzedin al Qassam Brigades. Though ultimately one could argue that all three uprisings have brought meagre results for the Palestinians, all three did visibly and forcefully demonstrate that occupation was profoundly unpopular, and would not be tolerated cost-free for the occupiers.

Resistance and accommodation

In contrast to these attempts at resistance, victorious and doomed, the more typical Middle Eastern experiences of European colonialism and the patterns of reaction were more prosaic, characterised by a continuing relationship of both cooperation and struggle. This reflects the fact that colonial era politics was often mundane, local and short term in preoccupation. Local elites were as much likely to seek office, resources and title within an overall context of colonial rule, as to focus on the more long run and strategic objective of national independence.

It is useful to distinguish between British and French styles of colonial management in the Middle East. France was an interventionist state, which believed in its own civilising mission, and sought to transform the values as well as the power relations of its colonial territories. Britain by contrast was the great sub-contractor of colonial control. It did so in Iraq and Transjordan with the Hashemites. It did so to the separate and discrete communities of Arabs and Jews in Palestine. In Egypt, politics after 1922 was a triangular relationship, featuring the British ambassador, the palace and the political class, dominated by rural landowners that sat in parliament. Though governments and elites sought to maximise their powers and bolster their legitimacy by distancing themselves from the colonial actor to which they owed their office in the first place, they were also part of the executive branch of a system that reproduced colonial control and an imbalance of power.

In Iraq, for example, King Faisal I was able to maximise his room for manoeuvre by playing off the British and the local elites. He would persuade the British to increase his political autonomy in order to ensure that there was no repetition of the violent events of 1920. To the local elites, he would argue that only the monarchy could maximise political and economic concessions from the British. It was only Faisal's early and untimely death in 1933 and the dynastic succession to an uninterested, naive and feckless younger generation that undermined this system and allowed the army to emerge as a political broker, with disastrous consequences long term.

Arguably, European colonialism's greatest success during this time was in the establishment, consolidation and long-term existence of the Hashemite Kingdom of Jordan. The original residual state, formed from the arid margins of what was not included in the surrounding states, Transjordan was created with poor potential, a mandate before it was even a country. A partnership of Hashemite leaders, more generally competent than in Iraq, a handful of canny British secondees, and some efficient Arab administrators and merchants turned this most unpromising venture into what is eighty-five years or more later still a member of the Middle East system of states.

Central to the success of this project was the creation of a political economy of sufficient size and inclusivity to give the main power groups an interest in its continuation. British budget transfers funded the creation of a public sector, employment and contracting opportunities quickly building a state-dependent bourgeoisie; Bedouin tribesmen were co-opted into the military; displaced Palestinian traders emerged to become its private sector businessmen. Jordan's value as a buffer state (in turn against Wahhabi and then Israeli expansionism) encouraged other countries to meet the external subsidy payments, once the relationship with Britain had waned in the mid-1950s. The relationship was not without its dissonance, especially during the 1920s. But these disagreements were often about the pace, direction and nature of institutional development than about power itself.

Meanwhile, in the Gulf states politics progressed in a similar way to the Jordanian case. The first century of the British presence, which had been marked by a balanced relationship between highly unequal actors, gave way to growing intervention in domestic affairs, but one which, as in Transjordan, was usually carried out by a small presence with a light touch. Where there was significant British intervention this was either done because of wider great power strategy or because of the factionalism of local politics that attempted to enlist British support.

A good example of both these factors operating together could be seen in Kuwait at the turn of the twentieth century. Britain was concerned at the attempts by Imperial Germany to use the Ottoman Empire as a Trojan Horse through which to threaten its interests in the Middle East. The Berlin–Baghdad Railway had projected German power on the ground. Plans to extend the railway to Basra on the northern shores of the Gulf, offered the prospect of British and German colonial interests bumping up against each other on the ground. Britain sought to head off this manoeuvre by creating a firewall in the northern Gulf, by emphasising the separate nature of Kuwait from the governorate of Basra in today's Iraq. In order to do this the British were drawn into intra-Kuwait ruling family politics, as different interests sought to play up the competing external powers as a way of strengthening their position within the ruling Sabah family.

Through judgement and luck, the British increasingly hitched their fortunes to the man who many regard as the real founder of Kuwait as a state, Amir Mubarak al-Sabah, popularly known as 'Mubarak the Great'. He adopted the strategic position of the British in order to face down his rivals domestically, whom he removed in a swift and bloody putsch in 1899. The success of his coup d'etat ensured that he became the undisputed ruler of Kuwait. He would rule in close association with Britain, before his death in 1915.

While Britain's position was generally that of a favoured ally among the states of the Trucial Coast in the early to mid twentieth century, this was not uniformly the case. The island state of Bahrain is a polity that differs in some crucial respects from the other smaller entities on the Gulf shore. While the latter tend to be small, relatively ethnically homogeneous and dominated by systemic politics, Bahrain is an altogether edgier case. With a majority Shia community coexisting with a Sunni regime, a tradition of rights-based activism, large inflows of foreign workers (before the phenomenon grew in the region) and periodic bursts of street-focused political protest, the politics of Bahrain have been spasmodically tempestuous by the subregion's standards.

The main face-off between the British and the mass of the population on the island came in the 1930s, when local activists struggled over an extended period of time for the right to establish trade unions. The British-backed Khalifa regime opposed this demand. Increasingly, the regime looked to the Indian subcontinent for workers to man the nascent local industries, thereby under-cutting the indigenous workforce. This was the period of the creation of a labour surplus in Bahrain, a situation that still prevails on the island, and one which continues to give the regime the whip hand. Britain's refusal to grant union rights to key parts of the local workforce inevitably increased the political stakes and resulted in the growth of anti-colonial activism. Though Bahrainis eventually received the right to form their own syndicates, full independence did not come until 1971. Tensions between the regime and the marginalised Shia majority re-emerged in the 1990s, and continue spasmodically to the present day, when the tussles are over representative politics. Bahrain remains the most turbulent of the various smaller Gulf states.

The final years of the Ottoman Empire saw the beginnings of the emergence of particularistic ethno-nationalism, with

Turkish nationalism in the forefront of the trend. It would increasingly be in the name of these new national conscious-nesses that the anti-colonial struggles would be framed. The stories of anti-colonial resistance are heroic ones. They lose little in the countless retellings, apart perhaps from an approximation to fact. The figures associated with them are revered in their countries today. In most cases, notably in Iraq and Palestine, these were the stories of noble failures. In some cases they even hastened the emergence of a dependent colonial relationship, such as Egypt in the early 1880s. Of the first wave, only in Turkey was there a mass, anti-colonial nationalist movement capable of militarily resisting the great powers of the day and their regional surrogates. Three decades later the Algerian people would replicate this national stand, but with much higher casualties. In many cases, after an initial period of uneasiness, the relationship between the colonial powers and the local elites became a complementary, even a cosy one. This typified the experience of the Gulf states, but even extended to Jordan in the Levant. It would require the further weakening of the European colonial powers during the Second World War to render the Euro-colonial overhang untenable, and speed the pathway for widespread independence.

3
Independence

If the period between 1882 and 1920 had been the era of European colonial expansion in the Middle East, and the period between 1921 and 1945 had been the period of resistance, the latter had been almost completely unsuccessful in delivering up free, sovereign, independent entities. Only republican Turkey could have been said to qualify for this description. It is to the period between 1945 and 1971 that the peoples of the region would have to wait for the era of decolonisation and the creation of an autonomous state system. When it came, like sub-Saharan Africa, change was both overwhelming and turbulent, a result of the weakness of states, the welling up of the forces for social transformation and a prevailing atmosphere of chaos in the region.

Formal decolonisation

The Middle East's first experiences of political independence were narrow, limited, and largely irrelevant to the ordinary people of the day. As local populations became more resistant to European control, London and Paris made a series of compromises, invariably struck with local elites. These were often articulated in the form of revised treaties, in which the Europeans tried to hold a modified line of control in return for largely gesture politics, especially on such crucial issues of principle as sovereignty and independence.

As time went on this relationship between colonial powers and indigenous elites shifted in favour of the latter. This was most obvious in the case of territories where the political control of the colonial power had collapsed entirely. In Libya by 1943 Italian control had disappeared, as the Allies finally defeated Field Marshall Rommel and the Axis powers in North Africa. French control of its mandates, Lebanon and Syria, effectively ended once the Vichy collaborationist regime was wound up, and as German control receded in the wake of the D-Day operations. France once liberated was, however, able to hang on in its North African possessions, the relinquishing of which would take some years yet to achieve.

Even where the loss of imperial control was less dramatic in the region, power relations were still running in favour of local elites. This resulted in some curious developments. In the likes of Egypt and Iraq, increased power simply accrued to the local dynasty, while colonial power either ebbed or was refocused strategically, as in the case of the concentration of British troops on the Suez Canal. In other parts of the region, relations became more symbiotic as instruments of domination were dismantled but personal ties of mutual respect and trust remained. In Jordan after independence, for example, local politicians from King Abdullah downwards remained inclined out of a habitual prudence to sound out the senior British representatives on major political issues. In both Jordan and the Gulf, Britain would remain an important component of regime power, through the turbulent 1950s and beyond.

Though local elites appeared finally to have inherited politically, following the long transition of the mandate period, this tableau would prove to be illusionary. Small in number, tainted by association with the colonial power, and having led a paper struggle against the Europeans rather than a Turkish-style experience of resistance and combat, the inheritor elites were actually more vulnerable than they appeared. Their wealth was primarily concentrated in the land that these large landowners in Egypt and Syria possessed, its static nature making it vulnerable to the expropriation of future rivals.

Social change

There was one other factor that was important in the fleeting nature of the old elite's momentary victory: the emergence of new social classes. Though less visible than the colonial engagement with Middle East elites, social transformation in the region was every bit as profound. It began with the long region-wide economic boom that saw the population of the Middle East rise by some 300% between 1800 and 1914, also partly owing to the virtual elimination of plague. Economic growth was particularly notable in the late nineteenth century, with Europe the engine. Regional output expanded, especially in the agriculture sector. In response to a succession of factors from industrialisation and demographic growth to war and reconstruction, Europe needed to buy increasing volumes of cereals from the Middle East. Though there were periods of recession, with the Middle East being affected as most places by the global slump of the 1930s, these were followed by further periods of rapid growth, as a result of war and reconstruction in Europe in the 1940s and early 1950s.

The expansion in trade in turn stimulated economic growth in the Middle East. With the region now divided into a plethora of states, the newly established taxation and tariff regimes helped resources accrue to the centre, thereby strengthening the process of state building. The hardening of power centres in turn stimulated the construction and real estate sectors. The new state centres began to suck in significant levels of rural to urban migration. For example, the Muslim Brotherhood in Egypt, the best known and largest mass Islamist movement in the region, was created in 1928 initially as a welfare-dispensing organisation concerned to ameliorate the plight of recent arrivals in the growing city of Cairo.

There was also an important expansion in education in the Middle East. As a result of the establishment of a primary school system, levels of literacy, especially among urban males, was growing, and with it income disparities. By 1920, a secondary school sector was beginning to emerge in the main cities of the region. There were even a handful of universities established by this time, with foreign educationalists playing a growing part. Ancient institutions, like al-Azhar in Cairo, were supplemented by younger, more modern and more dynamic bodies like Robert College in Istanbul and the American University in Beirut, founded in 1863 and 1866 respectively.

The outcome of all this was that regional society, though still overwhelmingly made up of rural, peasant farmers, was becoming increasingly dynamic. Towns were beginning to develop into large conurbations, and were less easily controlled. Economic roles were becoming increasingly differentiated, with the maturing signs of class formation, especially in populous, semi-urbanised states like Egypt. If an embryonic working class was beginning to emerge in the cities of Egypt, it was the lower middle class that was the rising class, more widely recognised across the region in the form of increasingly visible and mobile artisans and shopkeepers. This class grouping would increasingly be supplemented by the 'new middle class', that is to say a state bourgeoisie, dependent on the state as clerks, teachers, bureaucrats and officers for its future incomes. In short, the social base of political activism was expanding, making the search for and retention of power one that could no longer be confined to the rarefied social centres represented by chancelleries and palaces.

The military and national independence

A traditional elite and a rapidly changing society proved to be a combustible combination. What countries like Egypt, Iraq and Syria lacked was any recognised mechanism for the latter to shape, reform or at least soften the former. In the absence of effective procedures and channels for debate and exchange, the new governments of the region lacked adequate responsiveness. Moreover, they were quickly discredited, notably by the lamentable performance of the Arab armies, especially those from Egypt, Iraq and Syria and the 'Arab Brigade' controlled by the Cairo-based Arab League, in the first Arab–Israeli War, 1947–48. Given the largely peripheral nature of the new classes, society tended to lack the organised vehicles to bring about change. The one exception was the military.

The involvement of the military in the politics of the region was nothing new. For several Ottoman generations the Janissaries, an elite force loyal to the sultan, had been an important component of political control before briefly working as a rival power centre, governed by its own interests. Elsewhere in the developing world the military had already established itself as an arbiter of politics in much of Latin America. The army in Iraq had arguably become the newly emerging Arab region's first politicised military, filling the political vacuum left by the death of King Faisal I in 1933. In 1941 the Iraqi army had almost succeeded in carrying out an anti-British coup d'etat, in support of Rashid Ali al-Keilani. It was 1949, the year of the three coups in Syria, which heralded the arrival of the military as a formidable actor in the politics of a leading post-colonial Arab state, and as the leading institution for regime and leadership change.

Important though the Syrian experience was, it was still not era-defining. Syria was a weak state turned in on itself and wracked by factionalism. In many ways the Arab politics of the 1950s and 1960s could be defined as the struggle for the political soul of Syria. Even tiny Jordan joined in the competition over the fate of its larger northern neighbour in the early part of this period.

It was in Egypt, the largest and most populous of the Arab states, that the role of the military would become definitive in the form of the Free Officers Movement. In 1952 Egypt's middle-ranking officers led by Colonel Gamal Abdul Nasser brushed aside the regime of King Farouk, the latest and last of the Khedive-style rulers, associated with the bankruptcy and mismanagement of a century before, sending him into a gilded exile from which he would not return. The military elements

NASSER

Gamal Abdul Nasser was the most iconic Arab figure of the twentieth century. Tall, with film star good looks, Nasser bestrode the Arab regional stage between the mid-1950s and his death in 1970. Eulogised in print and song, and delivering rabble rousing speeches via the Voice of the Arabs radio station from Cairo, at the height of his powers Nasser was an irresistible advocate of Arab national self-assertion in the last moments of European colonialism. From lower middle class origins (his father was a postal clerk), Colonel Nasser embodied the social changes already well underway in the region. A leader of the Free Officers movement, he helped to sweep away the ailing *ancien régime* in Egypt through the coup of 1952. As President Nasser, he arguably stumbled on regional fame by breaking the arms supply monopoly of the Western powers by ordering Soviet weaponry. He acquired legendary status by emerging as the political victor of the Suez Crisis. Union with Syria saw Nasser at the height of his powers in 1958. But this proved to be illusory. The union fell apart in 1961. Soon after, Egypt became embroiled in a costly civil war in Yemen. Nasser's lowest point came with the total defeat of his armed forces at the hands of Israel in the 'six day war' of June 1967. If Nasser's early promise in the foreign policy arena had began well only to end in disappointment, the same could be said with respect to domestic governance. Nasser flirted with three experiments in insti-tution building during his time in power, the Liberation Rally, the National Union and the Arab Socialist Union. In spite of continuing high levels of popularity at home, Nasser never quite trusted trans-ferring real political power out of his hands. He therefore remained the personification of the charismatic leader in the contemporary Arab world. Nasser died of a heart attack aged only fifty-two, his funeral a public focal point for widespread national grief.

that had taken over were closer to and more attuned to the new rising social classes. Nasser himself was a member of the lower middle classes from upper Egypt; Anwar Sadat, his eventual successor, was from a village in the Nile delta.

The Free Officers came to power with a sense of the need for political change rather than any elaborate policy programme. They set about consolidating their position in power. Land expropriations of the former elite were a rare priority for the new government, born of the need to ensure that the political class of the preceding half century could not stage a comeback. Beyond that, the reformist verve of the country's new rulers soon petered out. Later, in his search for a dual mechanism of mobilisation and social control, Nasser would dabble with socialism. The Arab Socialist Union was established in 1962, and would fleetingly be his institutional legacy. Though he was to gain a reputation as a man of action, Nasser was neither a deep thinker nor an ideologue. It was personal power and its retention that animated him as a politician.

The Free Officers took power in Egypt at the beginning of what would become an age of military rule, especially in the Third World. In addition to Egypt, the military took over in Pakistan in 1958, in Indonesia in 1965 and in Ghana in 1966. This period predated the strong moral antipathy towards the idea of the military in power that exists across much of the world today. In the 1950s the armed forces were regarded as promising agents of developmental transformation: they had the discipline of the service; their unity appeared to transcend intra-country, parochial differences and hence symbolise the existence of nation; they were associated with technological innovation. Such reasoning proved to be flawed. In Egypt, as elsewhere, the military would be no more efficient than the civilian sector in running the country.

It was regional politics rather than the domestic field that would come to define the Nasser era. Nasser rather stumbled across this opportunity, rather than it being the product of coldly calculated strategy. The critical period straddled 1954 and 1956, in the course of which Nasser faced down the Americans, became a leader of the Third World, turned the Middle East into a Cold War arena and humiliated the British and the French, thereby ending London's pretences to be able to hang on as a great power in the region. It was little wonder that he became an Arab legend. That is until his luck ran out, and he crashed and burned, the victim of the same strategic intuition that had served him so well a little over a decade earlier.

In 1954 Nasser was an ambitious leader, who wanted to consolidate his position at home, and end the residual influence of the colonial powers that had so restricted Egyptian potential under the monarchy. To do this, he opposed British attempts to establish an anti-communist defence agreement, its best known form being the Baghdad Pact, seeing through this late imperial ruse to cling on to regional influence. To emphasise Cairo's political independence, Nasser side-stepped the Anglo-French-American monopoly on weapons transfers to the region, and bought Soviet arms via Czechoslovakia. This audacity created an Arab regional following, which he regularly addressed through the new technology of radio transmissions on the Voice of the Arabs (*sawt al-arab*). Nasser's boldness also turned him into a Third World celebrity, and he took a leading role in the emergence of the Non-Aligned Movement in 1955.

Nasser pursued developmental success at home through large public works projects. For a hydraulic state like Egypt, the plan of plans was to be the construction of the Aswan High Dam aimed at harnessing the waters of the upper Nile. Key to its completion was the financing of the project. Having agreed to fund the project, in a world of bipolarity the US now withdrew its support to penalise Nasser for his indulgence of Communism. Piqued and frustrated, Nasser responded by nationalising the Suez Canal (and would soon after turn again to the Soviets, as the only viable alternative for dam funding). As the tension ratcheted up, the French, the Israelis and the British (the latter no doubt encouraged by their success in another example of rolling back local nationalism, against Mossadeq in Iran) hatched a conspiracy to bring down Nasser. It was, however, shabby and ill thought through. It left the Egyptians with a massive political victory. The Egyptians proved capable of keeping the canal operational without the assistance of the 'white man'. The Anglo-French military intervention ran out of steam and logistical assets, especially once Washington had expressed its disapproval. President Eisenhower later insisted that Israel withdraw its invasion forces. With British troops out of Suez for the first time in a century, Nasser could claim that the Free Officers had completed a genuinely historic national revolution.

THE SUEZ CRISIS

The Suez crisis was the crucial trial of strength between a new regime in Cairo and the waning strength of the old colonial powers in the Middle East. That the outcome was a thundering political success for President Nasser and a humiliation for Britain in particular was the product of two things: that Egyptian self-confidence was high; that London was living in the past, both in terms of regional threat perceptions and its own post-war military and diplomatic capabilities. The status quo in 1956 had been established two decades earlier, when an Anglo-Egyptian treaty of alliance recognised Cairo's independence, but crucially short-changed it on sovereignty. Britain, which owned the Suez Canal Company, was to retain a military presence in the strategic Suez Canal zone and retained the right to defend the country in the event of attack. This historical anachronism was a tempting target for Nasser, as relations with the West in general deteriorated. The sudden withdrawal of US funding for the proposed Aswan High

THE SUEZ CRISIS (*cont.*)

Dam was met with Nasser's nationalisation of the Suez Canal. The reaction of Britain and France to this move was neuralgic, with the former's leader, Anthony Eden, viewing Nasser as another Hitler, who must be toppled. Britain's initial assumption that Egypt would be unable to keep the canal functioning was disproved in reality, thereby leaving London with a stark dilemma: either retreat or confrontation. Britain and France chose the latter, engaging with Israel in a secret and ultimately unconvincing conspiracy. Its basic premise was that the two colonial powers would intervene along the canal to keep warring Egyptian and Israeli forces apart, following an invasion by the latter, thereby maintaining access. Condemned by both superpowers and suffering from military overstretch, London and Paris were obliged to accept a ceasefire and the failure of their enterprise, thereby handing Nasser's Egypt a political victory.

Second wave of regime change

The outcome of the Suez crisis left Egypt as the regional leader of the Arab world. This reality was reflected in such institutions as the Arab League, which was based in Cairo, and whose secretaries-general were invariably Egyptian. Nasser would use this strength to innovate to his diplomatic advantage. Arab summit conferences were introduced in 1964. Egypt created the Palestine Liberation Organisation (PLO), initially as a tool of Egyptian foreign policy, in 1964.

With 1956 having demonstrated the strength and mobility of Israeli military power, Egypt warily concentrated on the Arab domain in order to force its advantage. With the small Gulf states out of the central orbit of the Arab world, and beyond the reach of Cairo radio, it was the pro-British states of the main Arab hinterland that were most vulnerable to the wave of radical regional politics. Numerous contemporary published sources believed that it would be the Hashemite dynasty in Jordan that would succumb first (and soon) during the onset of this internecine, regional strife. In reality it was Iraq where the most spectacular incidence of regime change would take place, in 1958. While it was Yemen on which the protracted and costly regional struggle would focus in the early to mid-1960s.

Jordan was presumed to be most vulnerable for three reasons. First, it was considerably smaller and weaker than all of its neighbours. Second, Jordan was an excellent example of the porous nature of the state system in the region. Radical Arab nationalist ideas as propagated by Egypt could easily enter the kingdom, through the airwaves, as a result of the undiplomatic provocations of Egypt's embassy personnel and through the actions of the country's ambitious, younger urban politicians, who felt that they could ride the tiger of Arab nationalism. Third, because of the realities of Jordan's geopolitics, located as the kingdom was among Egyptian-inspired destabilisation, Syria's chronic domestic instability to the north, Israeli power politics to the west, and Palestinians angered by dispossession and dispersal at home.

The confident predictions of the doom-mongers at times seemed persuasive. Jordan was regularly convulsed by street violence in the mid to late 1950s; most notably in 1955, as it flirted briefly with the prospect of membership of the British-inspired regional security organisation, the Baghdad Pact. These were followed by rumours and claims of attempted army coups in 1957 and 1958, the truth of which remain unclear to this day. But Jordan managed to survive this tumultuous period, battered, but still intact as a regime and as a state. It did so in part as a result of good fortune: King Hussein's dismissal of General Glubb, the former British officer commanding the Jordanian military, fortuitously preceded the Suez crisis and helped distance Amman from London at a crucial time. In part as a result of regime authoritarianism, political parties were banned in 1957 and troops regularly deployed on the streets in a riot policing role. And in part this was because Jordan's enemies were never quite able or so disposed to apply the killer blow.

While commentators feared for the Hashemite regime in Jordan, it was actually its dynastic counterpart in Iraq that was swept away in July 1958. Ironically, it happened while Iraqi troops were being deployed to the Jordanian border, in solidarity with its embattled cousin regime. In its haste to move the formations quickly and effectively, munitions in hand, the leadership in Baghdad forgot the lesson of 1952 in Egypt and the dangers posed by the military. Presented with the seat of power, open and unprotected, the Iraqi military in the form of one of the region's many imitative 'free officers' movements did not require a second thought.

In retrospect it was clear that the Baghdad regime had been on borrowed time since Suez. Together with the Jordanians, it was the regional regime most associated with the British. The British army had restored the Hashemites after the 1941 coup. Nuri Said, the Hashemite's most loyal retainer, was the epitome of an Anglicised Arab, with his tweed suits, Edwardian moustache and gold pocket-watch. Lest there be any doubt about it, the Egyptian media stoked the boiler of anti-regime sentiment. When the coup took place it was far from mere chance that the Baghdad mob headed for and sacked three destinations: the palace, the British embassy and Nuri's house.

The sudden convulsion of regime change also owed much to the shortcomings of leadership, since the death of King Faisal I. While Faisal had been shrewd and had taken to kingship as part of the responsibilities of high birth, his successors had nowhere near matched his calibre. His only son, Ghazi, was a shallow waster, who perished in a car accident. His son, the hapless Faisal II, was a minor during much of this time, and only eventually acceded two years before his ouster. He remained passive and innocent, in contrast to his cousin, the restless Hussein, in Jordan, who was determined to do whatever was necessary to keep his throne. For much of Faisal II's nominal reign authority was wielded by his uncle, and regent, Prince Abdulillah, a self-preoccupied and conceited man, whose peevish airs and graces had alienated Iraqis as Faisal I's patrician charm had won them over. Both uncle and nephew died in the hail of bullets which marked the start of the brutally unforgiving nature of failure that would afflict Iraqi leadership politics from then onwards.

Victorious, defeated

In 1958 it appeared as if the forces of Arab radicalism were poised to win a great victory. Free Officers were in power in Cairo and Baghdad, and Ba'thists in control in Damascus. British and American troops were fire-fighting, rushed to Jordan and Lebanon respectively to stabilise jittery regimes. The Algerian war of independence had brought down the Fourth Republic in France; complete colonial capitulation was just three years away. Pro-Nasserite 'liberal princes' in Saudi Arabia were complicating what was already a leadership riven by division. Furthermore, the Arab nationalists appeared to be consolidating their cause, as Syria's radicals appealed to Nasser for political union, a request that he could not refuse, leading to the creation of the United Arab Republic. In 1961 Iraq would threaten the newly independent, conservative state of Kuwait; it seemed as though the radical wave would at last reach the Gulf states too. The US's response in the shape of the Eisenhower Doctrine, whereby financial and other assistance would be forthcoming in combating Communism, grasped the sense of threat but had fixated on the wrong ideology.

Yet, in spite of this appearance, 1958 was actually the high watermark of radical politics. Within three years it was on the wane, with the radicals squabbling and Egypt distracted. In 1967 the Arab world was to suffer a crushing defeat at the hands of

Israel. With the fantasies of nationalist radicalism exposed, and Nasser a broken man, Egypt had little choice but to accept the realities of regional politics. If 1967 brought to an end the radical politics that had dominated the region since 1952, the period after 1967 was increasingly to be dominated by pragmatism and consumerism.

It was the assessment of 1958 which was misleading rather than realities on the ground. The union between Egypt and Syria, though the world accepted it at face value as the first stage in the restoration of the glorious, united Arab nation, was in fact a sham. Without any apparent hint of irony, Nasser treated Syria like a colony, appointing Egyptian regime figures to govern the various regions of his vassal entity. Resentment and ambition rapidly built up in equal measures among Syria's radical politicians, inexorably creating the conditions for a unilateral declaration of independence in 1961.

A gap rapidly emerged between the rhetoric and reality of power in Iraq after July 1958. Again, there were great hopes within militant circles that Iraq would join the UAR, creating a radical, nationalist wedge across the centre of the Arab world, prompting the smaller, dependent states of the region to succumb. Abdul Karim al-Qasim seemed to be a promising partner for such a venture, having been elevated to the head of the Iraqi free officers in the approach to the coup's implementation. Again, such expectations proved to be misconceived. Qasim's leading rival within the Iraqi free officers, Abdul Salam al-Arif, was already close to Cairo. If he were to survive and prosper in power, Qasim needed to look elsewhere for allies. Thus, he distanced Arif, sent him into exile in Europe, and stood out against Egyptian plans. In doing so, Qasim was playing to his strengths. With his father a Sunni Arab, and his mother a Shiite Kurd, Qasim appeared to be the composite Iraqi man. His very blood and sinews seemed to determine that he act like an Iraqi first. A mixture of personal ambition and the first stirrings of territorial state nationalism began to look strong enough to face down the potency of Arab nationalism.

By 1961 then the inexorable march of the Arab ranks suddenly looked less convincing. The cause of Arab unity and the forging of a central axis surged again in 1963, with the downfall of the regime that had rejected Nasser in 1961 and with Qasim's fall at the hands of a reinvigorated Arif. For all of his earlier playing of the Egyptian card, Arif shared the disinclination of the 1958 Syrians simply to hand over Iraq to Egyptian tutelage. In Damascus, it soon became clear that the outcome of the 1963 coup was to be a Ba'thist regime, nationalist rivals to the region's Nasserists. With radical prospects in the end only flickering in 1963, the utopian nature of the pan-Arab project was becoming clear, especially when the fortunes of the Yemeni civil war, which had commenced a year before, were taken into account.

In 1962 the traditional head of the underdeveloped and tribalised northern part of Yemen, the Imamate, had been overthrown in a military coup. Rather than meekly accepting the outcome, Saudi Arabia and other states with comparable traditional and pro-Western regimes, notably Jordan, joined ranks to try to restore Imam Badr. They did so most importantly because of the spread of regime change into the Arabian Peninsula, the heartland of traditional politics. In order to ensure that regime change was not rolled back in Yemen, Nasser felt duty bound to rally in support of the republicans, an early example of the Egyptian leader being entrapped by his own swashbuckling advocacy of regional political change. Egypt's support was not half-hearted. By 1965, some 55,000 men from the elite ranks of the Egyptian army had been committed to the cause. A combination of an organised and well-resourced enemy, a geographically very difficult terrain and the fact that Egypt's Saudi rivals were playing at home all added to the impossibility of a swift victory. This was in spite of Cairo's use of chemical weapons, the first such weaponised use of non-conventional weapons in the Middle East region. Egypt's Vietnam would ensure that Cairo would face the Israelis in the 1967 June war at a significant military disadvantage.

The Yemen civil war proved to be the centrepiece of what Malcolm Kerr has famously called 'the Arab Cold War', a struggle between radical nationalist and traditional states in the region. It was also a classic case of conflict by proxy, with Egypt and Saudi Arabia engaged in a struggle for regional hegemony through their local allies in Yemen. It was, furthermore, an early harbinger of a broader Cold War proxy conflict, the type of which would engulf such places as the Horn of Africa a decade and more in the future. Prior to the Yemen civil war the forces of pro-Western tradition were internally divided, externally embattled, and deeply suspicious of one another. For Jordan and Saudi Arabia the tension went back to the 1920s and the loss of the Hijaz by the Hashemites to the Al Saud. The Eisenhower Doctrine had stiffened Amman and supported it financially. The rising influence of Prince Faisal (leading to his accession as king in 1964) gave greater steel to the Saudi regime. At last the rival houses of Hashem and Saud had agreed to put aside their conflicting dynastic ambitions in favour of the strategic goal of resisting a radicalism that potentially threatened them both. The tide had at last been turned.

With regimes increasingly suspicious of ideological politics, and public opinion exhausted by the turmoil that they had brought, the atmosphere in the region from the 1970s was ripe for the partisan de-politicisation of government. Increasingly ministers across the region were drawn from among the ranks of technocrats, or selected according to primordial criteria, because of their ethnic, confessional, tribal or regional backgrounds, rather than their adherence to a particular body of ideas. The emphasis was more on the administration of countries than their political transformation. Politics had literally become a dirty word, especially in the rapidly expanding higher education sector of the Arab world's universities, where departments of law and administrative sciences became the alternatives of choice, and where a sanitised version of history and social sciences was taught if taught at all. The onset of rising oil prices, the resulting surge in oil rents and the preoccupation with developmentalism, the latest euphemistic alternative, saw a region replace a fixation with politics with a hunger for consumption.

Final flickers of nationalism

Defeat in the 1967 war and the passing of Nasser did not spell the complete demise of Arab nationalism. Regime change in Libya in September 1969 indicated that there was still some gas in the tank, as a precocious twenty-seven-year-old officer called Muammer al-Qadhafi led the overthrow. On-off over weeks, the conspirators were shambolic, but nothing like as much as the regime that they so easily brought down. The Sanussi regime of King Idris had become introspective and unresponsive, entirely wrapped up in its own machinations and oblivious to events elsewhere in the state. In spite of the presence of substantial numbers of US and British troops in the country, the former stationed at the gigantic Wheelus air base on the coast, the conspirators succeeded in seeing off the regime and then negotiating away the foreign presence.

Qadhafi positioned himself as the heir to Nasser. He famously refused to promote himself to a military rank in excess of that held by Colonel Nasser. He took on the restricted practices of the international oil companies before the heyday of the oil cartel, Opec, nationalising the country's oil operations in 1970. Incongruously, he railed against the very existence of a state, whose institutions he had just captured. He spoke stirringly of the creation of a 'state of the masses' (*jamahiriya*). His good looks, dark curly hair and brooding intensity made him as attractive a revolutionary figure as any unshaven, leather-jacketed student leader on the left bank in Paris.

Qadhafi proved in the end to be more peripheral eccentric than visionary leader. Publication of his political and economic philosophy, the 'Third Universal Theory', in his 'Green Books' showed his ideas to be pretentious and infantile. The creation of an all female bodyguard, exclusively comprised of nubile young women, owed more to vanity than gender equality. A handful of unity schemes, with Egypt, Sudan and even far away Syria, ended in disunity and recrimination. His sponsorship of violent Arab politics eventually led to mass murder as Pan-Am Flight 103 was blown to bits over the Scottish town of Lockerbie in 1988. Once disillusion and impatience with Arab politics had set in, Qadhafi became a notable patron of African liberation movements. His one success was Nelson Mandela, who loyally remains in his debt. His other friends, like the late insurgency leader Foday Sankoh in Sierra Leone, were responsible for bringing little but strife to their communities. Of Nasser and Qadhafi one is reminded of the famous paraphrase of Karl Marx: history repeats itself, first as tragedy second as farce.

Given the widespread fixation with elite politics, many of the social changes bubbling under during the inter-war years were ignored. Marked trends in population growth, education attainment and internal migration meant that the social landscape of most of the countries of the region was being rapidly transformed. It is puzzling in retrospect that so many of the players of the day, both indigenous and external, seem to have assumed that the conduct of politics could simply continue more or less as before. The formal repackaging of entities from colonial creations to states governed by local elites seemed to suggest that regimes had successfully negotiated the key transition. The short duration of the inheritor regimes in Egypt, Iraq and Syria, in great part undermined by their inability to prevail in Palestine and over the post-war order more generally, underlined just how shallow a presumption this had been.

When they came, the real national revolutions were turbulent affairs. The existing governing elites were changed; their support base was undermined; foreign policies were realigned. There was, in short, no way back for them. The Nasserite wave seemed to be unstoppable, as illustrated by its stunning political victory at Suez. This too proved to be an illusion, as the radical states jostled for status and the traditional regimes proved to be more durable than believed. The result was that the whole region was ripped in two. An Arab Cold War ensued every bit as icy and as edgy as its global variant. The Arab world turned in on itself, preoccupied with issues of identity and power. The civil war in Yemen during the early to mid-1960s proved to be the eye of the storm. The Arabs only veered away from this introspective and debilitating exercise in the mid-1960s. The basis for a belated pulling together was not, however, a sustainable one. Only by opposing Israel could Arab unity be generated. Such preoccupations omitted to consider the nature and strength of the state that it opposed, knowledge levels of Israel in the Arab world being virtually non-existent. The outcome was a total defeat in the 1967 war, and the fatal undermining not only of Egyptian and Nasserite leadership but even of Arab nationalism itself.

4

Conflict

Over the last six decades the Middle East has come to be inextricably associated with the theme of inter-state conflict. The impression is easily given that the Middle East is awash with conflict, enduring and bloody. This is somewhat misleading. Much of the region has never seen appreciable levels of conflict. Where inter-state conflict has taken place, it has tended to be limited in scope, concentrated mainly on the Israeli rim, and relatively brief. Only the Iran–Iraq War, 1980–88, with its one million casualties and resonating with the trench warfare of the First World War, departs from this generalisation.

In spite of the devastation of the Iran–Iraq War, and what is now referred to as Gulf Wars I and II, it is the various Arab–Israeli conflicts that most think of when they associate the Middle East with conflict. This is understandable for two reasons. First, the issue of longevity. Though the Arab–Israeli conflicts have tended to be short-lived in duration themselves, they have punctuated a period of some sixty years, from the war of state creation (or non-creation for the Palestinians) in 1948–49 to the Israel–Gaza twenty-four day war in winter 2008–9. Indeed, if one defines the struggle as one between rival nationalisms, rather than states or aspirant states as such, one can easily date it as spanning more than a century. Second, it is a conflict that has had a significant impact on the overall politics of the Middle East, from Palestinian dispossession and occupation in 1948 and 1967 respectively, through to the struggle for the control of the regions' weaker entities in Jordan, Lebanon and Palestine more recently.

Israeli–Palestinian conflict

Historically, the Arab–Israeli conflict has existed on two levels. The first, the Israeli–Palestinian level, was dominant before 1948 and has been again since 1993. The second, the conflict between Israel and the Arab states, particularly the former's neighbours, was dominant between 1948 and 1973. Over the remainder of the period, between 1973 and 1993, the levels were of equal or fluctuating importance.

The Israeli–Palestinian conflict has had two phases to it, and may be in the process of entering a third. Initially, the conflict was between two peoples for control over a single territory, the land of historic Palestine, west of the River Jordan to the Mediterranean Sea. These two groups were the Jewish people who had emigrated to the Holy Land or actively supported this migration, and the Palestinian Arabs who were the long-standing inhabitants of the area. This struggle began in the 1890s with the emergence of the Zionist movement, led by Theodor Herzl, and intensified during the 1920s, leading to the first major outbreak of violence over the issue at the end of that decade.

ZIONISM

Zionism is the national liberation ideology of the Jewish people. It emerged in the 1890s in continental Europe in response to the anti-semitic persecutions of Russian and Eastern European Jewry, and scandals like the Dreyfuss Affair in France. The underlying assumption of the Zionist movement was that Jewish assimilation was not possible even if desirable, a point endorsed by the Nazi Holocaust, which even targeted Jews on the grounds of race rather than solely religion or beliefs. Secular in its origins, at first the Zionist movement pursued the goal of a Jewish refuge without a particular geographical preference. Sites in South America and East Africa were considered. However, historical connections to the

ZIONISM (cont.)

land of Palestine gave focus to the movement. Though Herzl died in 1904, his initiative was already taking off. Strong institutions like the Jewish Agency, established to purchase land in Palestine, followed. Jewish emigration to Palestine stepped up in the 1920s. In the 1930s and 1940s the Jewish community in Palestine (*Yishuv*) increasingly acquired the appearance of an embryonic state, with a police force and an army (*Hagannah*). When the Jews of Palestine realised statehood in the form of Israel in 1948, Zionism became the official ideology of the state. Its values underpinned such articles of faith as the Law of Return, which provided for automatic citizenship to any Jew choosing to emigrate (*aliyah*) to Israel. Since the 1980s, a debate has been kindled in Israel about the future need for and nature of Zionism, especially as Israel itself seemed to have entered a new phase of political maturity.

The second dimension to the Israeli–Palestinian conflict came after both peoples had reluctantly accepted that they were unlikely ever to have a monopoly over the whole of the contested territory. Thus the conflict morphed into a struggle for mutual recognition and acceptance, and some form of territorial compromise. This struggle emerged fitfully between the early 1970s and the late 1980s. At the outset, the Israeli prime minister, Golda Meir, had famously refused to recognise that such a people as 'the Palestinians' even existed. By the end, it was still actually illegal for Israeli citizens to meet with members of the Palestine Liberation Organisation (PLO), the movement for Palestinian national aspiration. By 1989, however, the PLO had formally recognised the existence of the state of Israel and had 'renounced terrorism', in conformity with a form of words drafted by the Americans. A dialogue had been established between the organisation and Israel's closest supporter, the US.

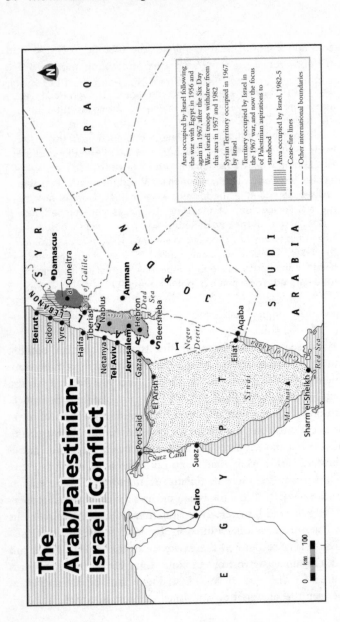

The Arab/Palestinian-Israeli Conflict

Area occupied by Israel following the war with Egypt in 1956 and again in 1967, after the Six Day War. Israeli troops withdrew from this area in 1957 and 1982

Syrian Territory occupied in 1967 by Israel

Territory occupied by Israel in the 1967 war, and now the focus of Palestinian aspirations to statehood

Area occupied by Israel, 1982-5

Cease-fire lines

Other international boundaries

Israelis and Palestinians took part in the October 1991 Madrid peace conference. In September 1993, following another peace breakthrough in Oslo, the leaders of Israel and the PLO shook hands on the White House lawn in Washington DC, signalling publicly their mutual recognition.

The 1990s represented the high watermark of hope for a historic settlement between the two sides. Bilateral peace negotiations defined the period between 1993 and 2000. However, with the final collapse of the process, and the commencement of the second Palestinian uprising (*intifada*) in September 2000, the relationship has since soured. The eight years that have elapsed have been dominated by a surfeit of violence and a dearth of peace-making, with the December 2007 Annapolis summit finally but unconvincingly breaking this dismal run. Suicide bombings, oppressive restrictions on the movement of people and goods, targeted assassinations which have killed senior Palestinian political leaders, the killing of an Israeli cabinet minister, the construction of a barrier to separate the two peoples, home-made and modern rocket attacks on Israel from Gaza, and imprisonment without trial have dominated this period. Both sides have been perpetrators and targets. Neither side has a monopoly on virtue. Both sides have their narratives of injustice, suffering and victimhood. If these narratives had been cathartic in the pre-1990s and muted during the period of intense peace-making, they have since returned with a destructive force that is blinkeredly used to legitimise acts of destruction.

In January 2006 the Palestinian Islamists of Hamas won elections to the de facto Palestinian parliament, and consequently formed a government. International pressure led to its brief replacement with a unity government. But this collapsed when Hamas seized power in Gaza in summer 2007, with Fatah consolidating its grip on the West Bank. Fatah, the Palestinian faction formerly led by Yasser Arafat, and the dominant part of the PLO since the late 1960s, had lost its monopoly on

Palestinian representation for the first time in some thirty-five years. The consequences of this split have been disastrous for the Palestinian people, with Hamas and Fatah ruling their respective fiefs with rods of iron.

Such developments have placed the future of Israeli–Palestinian peace-making in doubt. Hamas has refused to recognise the legitimate existence of the state of Israel or to accept agreements that had been forged in the past between the two sides. The best that Hamas was prepared to do was to offer a long-term ceasefire (*hudna*). This would allow it potentially to consolidate its position on the ground, pending by implication the reopening of armed activity at some stage in the future or giving time to its supporters to come to terms with Israel's existence, depending on one's point of view. If the previous three decades appeared to have been marked by a growing mutual acceptance by the two peoples, the new millennium seems to have been characterised by a deepening mutual disdain and intolerance, as illustrated by the 2008–9 war in Gaza. The very real danger exists that Samuel Huntington's 'clash of civilisations' will come to define a third phase to the Israeli–Palestinian struggle.

YASSER ARAFAT

Arafat (*nom du guerre*: Abu Ammar) came to prominence in 1968, as his Fatah organisation took over the PLO and made it into an organisation independent of direct influence by the Arab states. From that moment onwards, Arafat's face – unshaven, grinning, with a black and white headscarf (*kaffiyeh*) round his neck, worn over his olive green fatigues – became the face of the Palestinian national movement. It was in such a guise that he addressed the UN General Assembly in 1974, speaking of a gun in one hand and an olive branch in the other; and that he signed the Declaration of Principles with Israeli leaders on the White House lawn in

YASSER ARAFAT (*cont.*)

September 1993. Elected president of the newly created Palestinian Authority in 1996 it seemed that 'the old man', as he liked to be known before he became old, would lead his people into the political promised land of independent statehood. Yet by 2000 it had all gone wrong. Arafat resisted US and Israeli bullying during peace negotiations at Camp David II, to return home a hero. However, launching a second Palestinian uprising, which resulted in wave upon wave of suicide attacks, was a grave mistake. The Israelis never trusted him again, and he was rushed to his death-bed in Paris from a much diminished base in Ramallah. Arafat was clearly a flawed figure: elliptical; preoccupied with tactics; not entirely reliable; and with a weakness for cronies. But, as 'Mr Palestine', the face of the Palestinian people, he was the one man who could have signed a full peace with Israel and made it stick. With that in mind, Israel allowed its exasperation with the man to cloud its judgement on where its best interests actually lay.

The wider Arab–Israeli struggle

If the Israeli–Palestinian struggle lies at the core of the historic conflict on the ground, it has existed within a broader context of Israeli–Arab antagonism. There have been three fully blown Arab–Israeli wars: 1948–49, the war for Israel's creation; June 1967, the war that transformed the conflict from one of existence to one of territory; and October 1973, the Arabs' political war, aimed at engaging American mediation rather than the destruction of Israel. In addition, there have been any number of more limited, though significant engagements. These have included: 1956, and Israel's collusion with colonialism at Suez; 1968, and the Battle of Karameh, the first set-piece engagement against any Arab force that Israel had failed to win in twenty years; 1968–70, and Egypt's 'war of attrition', when

Cairo refused to accept the status quo of the loss of its territory; 1982 (and its limited precursor in 1978), Israel's invasion of Lebanon; 1993, 1996 and 2006, and Israel's three limited military forays into Lebanon.

The conventional view of the Arab–Israeli wars was, until the early 1980s, in conformity with the David and Goliath analogy. Israel was widely seen as small and vulnerable, struggling against the odds to secure its very survival amid a sea of enemies. The Arabs were seen as monolithic, unreasonable and hell-bent on Israel's destruction. The advent of the 'new historians' in Israel, academics like Avi Shlaim who have offered a different narrative, has tempered this view. Israel was not out-gunned, out-manned or out-supplied in 1948, as is often supposed; in late 1948/early 1949 in the third phase of the war the Israeli army moved purposely to increase the territory controlled by the new state, well beyond the land assigned to it under the UN territorial partition of historic Palestine in 1947. Moreover, the Arab side was not a single entity but four. It was riven by dynastic tensions and traditional geostrategic competition, which climaxed with a Jordanian land-grab of the remaining territories designated for an Arab state, soon to be known as the West Bank. In short, Israel's enemies were seldom well coordinated or effective. The most eloquent verdict on the Arab states in the 1948–49 war is that within three years, two of them, Egypt and Syria, had undergone regime change, in part a result of these battlefield debacles.

Though, like its leader, David Ben-Gurion, Israel was pugnacious during the 1950s, its prospects were far from certain. At its narrowest, the distance between the Green Line, delineating Israel from its Jordanian neighbour, and the Mediterranean Sea was only nine miles. Arms supplies were limited in the early to mid-1950s. It would not be until the Johnson presidency after 1967 that the US would become an increasingly supine strategic supporter of Israel. Eisenhower's impatient insistence on Israel's withdrawal following the occupation of the Sinai in 1956 is testament to a more robust American posture in an earlier era. Meanwhile, many Palestinians languished in refugee camps in Jordan, Lebanon and Syria, waiting for Nasser and the Arab states to act on their behalf. Deterred by the memories of 1956, Nasser concentrated on the Arab political sphere, as the logic of states rather than ideological rhetoric increasingly drove Egyptian policy. As the frustration of the refugees increased, a low intensity war emerged against Israel's borders perpetrated by various Palestinian guerrilla groups from the late 1950s through the 1960s.

Given the care with which Egypt avoided war with Israel for a decade to 1967, the renewed outbreak of hostilities remains something of a puzzle. Richard Parker, in his exhaustive research on the June war, has placed the causes of the conflict at the door of miscalculation. Certainly there were enough parties in the approach to war for this to be plausible. Other parties were happy to play their own narrow game without due consideration for the train of events. Arab perceptions of Israel and the US were especially flawed.

The lurch to war began with faulty Soviet intelligence being conveyed to Cairo about an imminent Israeli attack on Syria. Though the veracity of this misreporting was debunked, it helped create a febrile atmosphere of fear and suspicion. Crude propaganda from Damascus and Amman ridiculed Nasser's caution, provoking him into dismissing the presence of a UN force, stationed in the Sinai to keep the peace since 1957. Once embarked on the road to escalation, Nasser seemed unable or unwilling to turn back. He announced that the Straits of Tiran, giving access to Israel's Red Sea port of Eilat, would be closed, a move that Israel had already declared to be a *casus belli*. Israeli prime minister, Levi Eshkol, a dove trying to resist intra-cabinet pressures to appoint the hawkish Moshe Dayan as defence minister, sent out conciliatory signals. However, these were misinterpreted as weakness by the Arab side, which became more wedded to the instrument of war. In an emotional policy flip flop, Jordan's King Hussein threw in his lot with Nasser at the last minute, perhaps for fear of the domestic backlash if he remained aloof. Faced with this escalation, Israel acted pre-emptively. The promises made to Nasser by his old friend and Egyptian army head, Field Marshall Abdul Hakim Amr, about the strength of the Egyptian forces were exposed as empty posturing. Israel won the war on the first day through its destruction of the Egyptian air force on the ground. With air supremacy, victory in a land war on three fronts was only a matter of a short period of time.

For the Arabs, Egypt lost the Sinai, Syria the Golan Heights and Jordan the West Bank. A more comprehensive victory is difficult to conceive of. There were many positives that came out of the war. Arab chauvinism, the dominant ideology in the region of the previous decade and a half, was thoroughly discredited, freeing the way for the growth of territorial state nationalism, which would help to consolidate the individual Arab states. Nasser himself was chastened by the events, and embarked upon a more realistic diplomatic course, the eventual outcome of which would be a peace treaty with Israel under his successor a decade or so later. King Hussein of Jordan drew the lesson that the military defeat of Israel was unfeasible, and dedicated the rest of his life to the diplomatic process. A more pragmatic leadership would even emerge in Syria three years later, with Asad's 'Correctionist Movement'. If Israel was now to be less threatened, the acquisition of new territory, it seemed at the time, would also make it more secure.

But if 1967 was in many ways a good thing it was too much of a good thing. Rather than returning occupied land in exchange for a durable and institutionalised peace with its neigh-bouring states, Israelis became intoxicated by victory. Some saw it as a gift from God. Others believed the hubris of Israel's military invincibility. The transformation of the US, one of the world's two superpowers, into an increasingly uncritical partner, weakened international diplomacy and reduced the incentive for Israel to cash in its newly gained political chips. Worst of all, Israel failed to appreciate exactly what it had got. For right wing Zionists and some religious Jews Israel had gained the most valuable parts of the land of Israel (*Eretz Israel*); after-all, if the Jewish people did not inhabit biblical Jericho, Jerusalem, Hebron and so on what right did they have to control the coastal plain? But they and Israel's mainstream leaders failed to appreciate that the West Bank and Gaza did not come uninhabited. Far from it. The Occupied Territories came with almost one million Arab Palestinians, now located next door to a Jewish population in Israel proper of only 2.4 million in size. The dilemma of what to do with these unwelcome Palestinians would underpin the emerging tension between the hitherto harmonious two core values of Israel, Jewishness and democracy. The beginning of the debilitating moral cost of occupation had begun. The 'war of the wombs', in which Israelis and Palestinians would anxiously chart their rate of natural population growth, was to follow in an effort to 'create facts' on the ground.

Egypt at least did succeed in forcing the Israelis to consider making peace. An audacious and well rehearsed attack in October 1973, during which the Egyptian army crossed the Suez Canal, succeeded in restoring some precious national self-esteem. Israel's military supremacy was undermined by its intelligence failure to foresee the attack. The fact that Israel ended with the upper hand on the battlefield disguised its massive reliance on the US's resupplying of hardware lost in the first phase of war. But the 1973 war was much more about politics than military success. Israel's existence was never threatened, but it did come to realise that only through Egyptian participation could Israel be defeated in a conventional war. With Egypt's deteriorating economy demanding peace-making in Cairo,

Anwar Sadat took the courageous and unprecedented step of visiting Jerusalem in November 1977, where he addressed the Israeli parliament. It was the sort of political theatre that Sadat was good at. It helped to ignite a process that led to the Camp David Accords, brokered by US President Jimmy Carter, and which resulted in a full bilateral peace treaty and the restoration of the whole of Sinai to Egyptian sovereignty. Sadat's only crime was to act according to state interests, ignore wider Arab and Islamic feeling, and make a separate and unilateral peace with Israel. It would cost him his life, gunned down by militant Islamist elements in the Egyptian army, during the annual victory parade in Cairo in October 1981.

Though the accords provided nominally for other Arab participation, notably by the Palestinians and Jordan, the process came too soon for the other protagonists. Egypt was vilified in the Arab world and the seat of the Arab League relocated to Tunis. However, through the course of the 1980s it would be the other Arab states that would come round to the Egyptian position, rather than vice versa. By 1989 the Arab League was back in Cairo, and the PLO was pursuing a serious peace process. All major Arab states were present at the US–USSR sponsored October 1991 Madrid peace summit, including Syria. Jordan was to conclude its own separate peace with Israel in October 1994, but only after Arafat had signed a Declaration of Principles for peace with Israel in 1993, thereby unintentionally giving political cover to King Hussein's successful peace aspirations.

If the 1970s and the 1980s may be seen as a period when the Arab–Israeli conflict moved decisively in the direction of peace, the major discordant note was Israel's 1982 invasion of Lebanon, the year that international public opinion deserted the Israelis for the Palestinian cause. It was an unnecessary and misconceived war that has done more to undermine Israeli security than anything else. As such, it was the brainchild of the Israeli right, more particularly the two leading lights of the Likud government, prime minister Menachem Begin and defence minister Ariel Sharon, aided by a hawkish chief of staff, Rafael Eitan. The aim of the invasion was twofold: first, destroy the PLO, which had its political as well as its military infrastructure in Lebanon; second, manipulate Lebanese domestic politics to bring about another bilateral peace agreement, in this case between Israel and the Maronite right.

Three months and around 18,000 Lebanese fatalities later, the Israelis did bring about the managed expulsion of the PLO from Lebanon. Ironically, this had the opposite effect to the one desired. Instead of undermining the PLO as a regional player, the Israelis strengthened it as a political actor. By removing the last territorial base from which the PLO could attack Israel there was no realistic alternative for the organisation but to throw in its lot with a diplomatic strategy. The PLO could now credibly position itself as an actor responsible enough to claim sovereignty over the occupied territories that the Israeli right valued so highly. The massacre of some 1200 Palestinian refugees in the Sabra and Shatilla camps in Beirut at the hands of Maronite militiamen and under the noses of the Israeli occupiers, added to a wave of world sympathy for the Palestinians. As for a separate peace with the Lebanese state, this proved to be a fantasy. Syria and its Lebanese allies, particularly the Shia groups, Amal and Hizbollah, demonstrated the de facto veto that they wielded over Lebanese political developments. The assassination of the Maronite president-elect, Bashir Gemayel, and mass casualty suicide attacks against American targets in early 1993 saw off the manoeuvre.

Two decades of Israeli involvement in Lebanon, with its patchwork of confessional communities and multiple factions, has proved time and again how little Israel understands the region, and what a novice it is when it comes to the art of managing Arab politics. After its failure in Beirut, Israel allowed itself to be harried in Lebanon for three years before withdrawing to a 'security zone' in the south. It was subsequently harassed for fifteen years in the south, allowing its enemy, Hizbollah, to legitimise and entrench itself as the Lebanese national resistance against 'the Zionist invader'. Losing around twenty-five service-men killed per year, Israel was eventually persuaded to leave the south of Lebanon in May 2000. The ragtag Lebanese allies that it left in its stead collapsed in quick time in the face of the unfulfilled prospect of Hizbollah retribution. With the credibility of the Israeli army and its strategy of deterrence seriously under-mined, Palestinian radicals transposed the Lebanese case to their context: all they needed to do, it was reasoned, was to force Israeli concessions through killing Israeli citizens. The suicide attacks and home-made rockets followed. Israel's forays back into Lebanon in the 1990s and in 2006 were forlorn efforts to reassert control. Political disasters all, they served to rally support behind Israel's enemies, notably Hizbollah and Hamas, and to underline the Jewish state's vulnerability to asymmetric warfare.

The Iran–Iraq war

The Iran–Iraq war, by contrast, was anything but asymmetric. It was the equivalent of two heavyweight boxers slugging away over eight long years. Eventually both sides fought each other to a standstill. In one corner was the Islamic Republic of Iran, a new regime established after the popular tide had swept away the monarchy. The war of revolutionary zeal, like France in the 1790s, was a convenient way of settling power struggles at home at a time of domestic turbulence. The new regime could then unite in the causes of exporting the Islamic revolution, freeing the oppressed and ultimately liberating Jerusalem. In the other corner was the Iraq of Saddam Hussein, a brutal dictatorship, a majority of whose people could be considered to be oppressed. Baghdad both feared the ramifications of the Islamic revolution, standing as it did between Iran and Jerusalem, and spied an opportunity to exploit the revolutionary turmoil next door. It was a monumental act of miscalculation from which the leadership of Saddam Hussein would never recover.

Baghdad exploited some random Iranian mischief making and invaded its eastern neighbour on 22 September 1980. The Iraqi strategy was to win some easy battlefield victories against an Iranian military weakened by the repeated purges of its officer class. At the all important political level, Iraq would 'free' the Arab population in south-west Iran from their Persian masters, take over the mantle of regional Arab leadership from an Egypt ostracised for its peace-making with Israel, and precipitate the downfall of the brittle new regime in Tehran. Instead, Iraq's conventional military push moved slowly, the invasion allowed the revolutionaries to rally support at home, and a series of debilitating battles wrecked the lives of Iran's Arabs around Ahwaz and Susangard. It was not long before the Iranians had gained the military initiative and Iraq was on the back foot.

By this stage it was already clear that this was not simply a conflict between two regional powers. With the revolutionaries having seized the American embassy in 1979, resulting in a 444-day hostage crisis, apparently pursuing an expansionist strategy across the Gulf waterway, and preaching the cause of political revolution across the Middle East, a tacit realisation began to spread that the Islamic republic could not be allowed to succeed. Thus, as early as 1981, the war had already evolved from a war of Saddam's vanity into a broad de facto alliance war for the containment of the Islamic revolution. Increasing numbers of countries, from the US and Israel to France and the USSR to virtually all of the Arab states (Syria mainly excepted) came around to viewing the conflict in these terms.

The containment strategy featured Iraq in 1982 withdrawing more or less to the international boundary and suing for peace. The UN Security Council supported such a move. Iran faced a fateful choice: accept the offer, maintain the moral high-ground and keep the pressure up for regional change, but possibly let Saddam off the hook; or keep up the military momentum, gamble on a region-transforming victory and 'punish the aggressor'. At the apogee of revolutionary passion, Iran chose the latter course. Iran was aided in its decision by a strong sense of outrage at international double standards in favour of the Arab side. The UN had not called for a return to international boundaries until Iraq had vacated Iranian soil. The organisation would be loathe to take a position against Iraq throughout the conflict, even over the documented use of battlefield chemical weapons against Iranian forces.

Though the two sides would fight one another to a standstill they were both very different in composition. With a population one-quarter of the size of its neighbour, and its economic and demographic centres vulnerable to Iranian attack, Iraq had been obliged to move to a full war stance in order to resist the onslaught. That meant that at any one time twenty-five per cent of its adult males were under arms. By contrast, with its population centres in the interior and fighting with a largely volunteer force, Iran was much less affected by the war, at least until the mid-1980s. If Iran had the 'natural' advantages in the struggle, the Iraqi side was evened up in two ways. One was the increasing resort to a qualitative edge in both conventional and non-conventional weapons to balance Iran's lower tech, mass manpower-based war effort. A second was the increasing intervention of third parties on Iraq's behalf. Moscow and Paris in particular made massive arms transfers to Baghdad, with the US helping in other ways, for example through extensive intelligence provision.

A series of Iranian offensives against Basra in the mid-1980s

AYATOLLAH KHOMEINI

If the Shah of Iran was widely despised by a range of opposition forces in the late 1970s, Ayatollah Ruhollah Khomeini was the man around whom most felt they could rally in the run-up to the 1979 revolution. In some respects this old man, already in his late seventies, with a long white beard, living in exile in Paris, was an unlikely revolutionary. A religious scholar for most of his life and latterly one of a handful of grand ayatollahs in Shia Islam, known for its predominantly quietist political tradition, Khomeini had not lived in Iran since 1964. He had, however, already by then established his credentials as a critical thinker and opposition activist through associating himself with the protests against the Shah's modernisation strategy of a year earlier. During a long exile in the Shia holy city of Najaf in Iraq, Khomeini developed his political creed of clerical power, rule by the Islamic jurist (*velayat-e faqih*) or Supreme Leader, a formula for his own eventual post-revolutionary pre-eminence. The death of a son in suspicious circumstances and a ham-fisted piece of black propaganda aimed at smearing his name increased a popular identification with Khomeini as a man who had really suffered at the hands of the Pahlavi regime. Khomeini became more practically involved in the unfolding revolution once expelled from Iraq, notably through the distribution of illicit tapes of his sermons. This tough but humourless man would help maintain a relentless pressure on the Shah rejecting compromise; when he returned in triumph to Iran in February 1979, after the Shah's flight, and was asked how he felt, he famously replied 'nothing'. Once established, the Ayatollah stood above the daily cut and thrust of policy-making in the Islamic Republic, but remained the ultimate arbiter of power. When the Iranian war effort was seriously ailing in 1988, it was to Khomeini that the senior regime figures went to sanctify a decision to end the conflict; he did so, but said that it was 'like drinking poison'.

drew attention to the limits of its military power. Iran had succeeded in capturing the important strip of land, the Faw Peninsula, but had failed to break through elsewhere. Moreover,

frustration was beginning to creep in, with increasingly desperate attempts to take the war to Iraq's supporters among the Gulf
states. Kuwait was subject to rocket attacks from Faw, for
example, while hundreds lost their lives during disturbances at
the pilgrimage in Saudi Arabia in 1987. Iraq and Iran exchanged
long range missile salvoes in a 'war of the cities'.

By 1987 it was clear that Iran could not win. An attempt to
internationalise the war had merely brought the US and others
directly into the conflict in order to protect 'neutral' shipping
bound for the Gulf states. Significantly, the stream of volunteers
for the Iranian war effort had dried up; the Iranian people had
lost the stomach for the war. Yet Iran baulked at accepting the
inevitable, and refused to agree to UN resolution 598, adopted
in August 1997, the main formula for an end to hostilities. It
would be a full year before Iran would finally accept the terms
offered. And then, with Faw lost, a rash of battlefield defeats, and
the mistaken shooting down of an Iranian civilian aircraft by a
US military vessel, the Iranian spiritual leader Ayatollah
Khomeini was only persuaded to endorse a cessation of hostilities when clear that the very long-term viability of the regime
was now in doubt. By August 1988 the guns had at long last
fallen silent.

The Iran–Iraq war was a monumental waste of men and
materials, a vaulting testimony to the cynicism of leaders, the
naivety of populations and the devastation that modern arms,
funded in unimaginable quantities by oil wealth, could wreak. It
was also a statement of the hypocrisy of the Muslim World,
contrasting its pious invocations that Muslim brothers should
never fight one another with the appalling reality spread over
time. It was also a testament to the crudeness of the high political calculations of external powers. Yes, the Iranian revolution
had been contained, but only at the expense of the profound
undermining of the balance of power in the northern Gulf.
With Iran introspective, and Iraq awash with armaments and

impatient to translate this superiority in hard power into tangible political and economic gains, the scene was ready for Iraq's disastrous invasion of Kuwait two years later. Not for the first time in the history of humankind, the Iran–Iraq war would require another war to undo its consequences.

Gulf War I

Having been under intense Iranian military pressure for six years, Iraq at the end of the Iran–Iraq War unexpectedly had the upper hand, both diplomatically and on the battlefield. However, this had been a pyrrhic' victory if a victory at all. Iraq had been thoroughly exhausted by the conflict, which had required the mobilisation of all the country's efforts to stave off the Iranian attacks. The Iraqi economy and society in particular had been affected, with a high degree of state indebtedness and no private sector to speak of. There was a strong will in the country to return to normality. But normality in such circumstances was difficult to rebuild. Such were the problems of absorption that Saddam Hussein even baulked at the demobilisation of the army to peace time levels. Politically testing times stood ahead.

The regime in Baghdad grappled with these problems for two years before serious frictions developed with some of the Gulf states, notably over their unwillingness to write off Iraqi debt generated during the war with Iran. Border tensions with Kuwait were further exacerbated by a raft of other problems, which included accusations that the emirate was horizontally drilling into Iraq's oil field at Rumaila, and that it was conspiring with the CIA to keep the oil price low and hence curtail desperately needed growth in the Iraqi economy. For Iraq, this action was tantamount to war by economic means. Demands for some $10 billion in aid from Kuwait were refused as the bilateral tensions escalated. As bad blood developed between the two erstwhile but arms-length allies, the attraction of an attack on the emirate must have seemed increasingly irresistible: around $100 billion worth of liquid and semi-liquid assets; control of Bubiyan and Wahba islands, commanding the approaches to Iraq's Gulf ports; wider access to the Gulf itself, in contrast to the narrow air-hole provided for by the mandate settlement. To Saddam's Iraq, Kuwait must have seemed like low hanging fruit.

Iraq attacked the emirate on 2 August 1990. After an unconvincing attempt to portray the invasion as a solidarity mission to help radical republicans in the Kuwaiti military, Iraq defended its actions on the ground of 'returning the branch to the tree'; that is to say reversing the British colonial separation of Iraq and Kuwait some eight decades before. The US-led international community perceived the invasion differently, regarding it as a gross violation of the UN Charter and the first time since 1945 that a sovereign state had ceased to exist as a result of the expansionism of a fellow member. A raft of international resolutions vilified the Iraqi action and punished it through a trade and financial boycott, which also prevented Baghdad from profiting from Kuwaiti investments abroad. In the first test of the post-Cold War era, the USSR lined up alongside the US, unwilling to jeopardise its new global friendships because of its somewhat choppy relationship with a regional power.

Washington's position was rendered unassailable by the cooperation it received from the majority of Middle Eastern states. Egypt proved crucial in organising a majority Arab League vote in condemnation of Iraq. The Gulf states, one of whose number had been so dramatically targeted, aided the US through the provision of military basing facilities and finance. Iran declared itself to be neutral in the emerging conflict, tantamount to leaning towards the US-led coalition. Even Syria, so often hard-line and nationalist in the past, fell in behind the pro-US Arab block, charging Saddam with recklessness. The nature of Saddam's growing predicament was best illustrated by those states which did remain at very least equivocal towards his position: at the UN Security Council Cuba and Yemen; within the Arab world marginal players, such as Jordan, the PLO and Sudan.

Having rushed a defensive force to Saudi Arabia, the Americans had curtailed Iraq's further expansionist options by September. In November the US decided to increase its military capabilities to offensive proportions, rising to half a million servicemen and women on the ground. Under US Secretary of State James Baker's leadership, the US line against bilateral negotiations with the Iraqis held better than could have been hoped for. Saddam vacillated over whether to use Westerners marooned in Iraq and Kuwait as hostages, ending up with the worst of both worlds: being vilified as a hostage taker but having released them all by the onset of intense hostilities.

On 17 January 1991 the US launched a thirty-eight day aerial bombardment in preparation for a land campaign. This succeeded in undermining the morale of the Iraqi troops. When the land war came it was swift and decisive, with a fast and accurate 'left hook' of an attack outflanking the Iraqi defences in the desert interior. With resistance in Kuwait crumbling, the land war lasted exactly 100 hours. Faithful to the limited nature of UN resolutions, President Bush senior declined to mount a push on Baghdad and the pursuit of regime change. That job would be assumed by his son some twelve years later, in a way that confirmed the wisdom of his father's self-restraint.

Though Iraq had been punished for its aggression and a sovereign, independent Kuwait restored, the US had not proved to be any more successful in achieving a balance of power in the northern Gulf. With Iraq steadily undermined by a sanctions regime that would last well over a decade, and most of its non-conventional weapons arsenal subsequently dismantled by UN specialist inspectors, Iraqi power was being seriously eroded in a way that could only favour Iran. The circumstances for the reemergence of Iran as a renewed force in the Gulf were now in place.

Gulf War II

The Clinton presidency was much more interested in the Arab–Israeli theatre, which it viewed as ripe for peace, than the Gulf. While the containment of Iraq was maintained as a strategy, the reality was the slow unravelling of sanctions. The return of Iraq, still led by Saddam Hussein, to the international community of states seemed only a matter of time. This prospect gave no joy to the Bush Jr presidency, with its neo-conservative outlook, which despised Clinton. The ideologues of the new administration wanted to transform Iraq into a democracy that would conclude peace with Israel and act as a shining beacon of good governance for the region. The international circumstances, however, were not propitious. This would change with 9/11.

The terror attacks in New York and Washington DC created a wave of international sympathy for the US. It provided a context for what would become the Bush Doctrine: forward, pre-emptive intervention to stymie such attacks as they were being planned. A successful US-led, international intervention brought down the Taliban regime in Afghanistan, which had given open sanctuary to Osama bin Laden and al-Qaida. Once the initial hostilities were complete in late 2001, senior members of the Bush administration focused on repeating the exercise in Iraq, even though there was no evidence of Baghdad's complicity in 9/11.

The Bush Jr administration adopted a strategy apparently similar to 1990: the US would undertake a decisive military intervention backed up by a multi-national coalition that would give it political cover, with the UN Security Council providing international legitimacy. Its implementation was a pale shadow of 1990, a reflection of the flimsiness of the justification and the disdain of senior administration figures. Crucially, Washington failed to secure clear UN backing. It even failed to convince all of its local allies, notably its fellow Nato member, Turkey. US forces secured an easy initial victory on the ground in March and April 2003. The Ba'thist regime was toppled. Saddam and his henchmen went underground, the former being apprehended in December 2003 and executed three years later. The US proved to be far more adept at a conventional military campaign. Over the following five years the US struggled to make much headway in terms of state building, reconstruction or the maintenance of civil peace.

On a number of key issues, especially early on, the US made the wrong calls, a reflection of an ignorance of Iraqi society, insufferable arrogance and administrative turf wars back in Washington. For example, the decision not to prevent an outbreak of looting and disorder immediately after the fall of the regime created a climate of lawlessness and insecurity in the country, which prompted Iraqis to look to primordial religious and tribal figures for protection and leadership. The decision to dissolve the Iraqi army left the country with no native force with which to keep the peace, and turned former Ba'thists against the US-led effort. Together with the militarisation of Iraqi factional politics and the emergence of an al-Qaida-inspired jihadist international, fear and violence escalated in the country. Meanwhile, the failure to discover any significant stockpiles of weapons of mass destruction, the *casus belli* cited by the US and its allies, turned the perception of the war into one of an oil obsessed, self-serving neo-imperialism.

Such was the confusion and unpreparedness of the US occupiers, that no fewer than three different attempts at governance building were made. The eventual key idea was to undertake a complementary process of institution creation and institution endorsement through referenda and elections. This worked in part: bringing most of the country's Shia majority into the political process, while providing considerable autonomy for the US's closest allies on the ground, the Kurds. But the US was much less successful with the other political communities in Iraq, notably the Sunni Arabs, who remained marginal at best to the process. Even the US's successes were debatable: Shia cooperation easily shaded into majoritarianism, the desire of the majority community to enjoy the spoils of its demographic preponderance; Kurds remained equivocal about the long-term desirability of rebuilding Iraq. The successes claimed for the occupation in 2007 resulting from a US military 'surge', notably a sharp reduction in jihadist violence and falling levels of Sunni Arab antipathy, drew attention to the low aspirations of an Iraq under American stewardship.

The Middle East is a region that is in many people's minds inextricably associated with violent conflict. This is hardly surprising. The fault-lines of ethnicity and sect and the ideologies that they have spawned are deep, though not necessarily deeper than they are elsewhere in the developing world. But the stakes are certainly high, whether calculated in terms of land, oil or threat perceptions. Conflict zones erupt periodically, notably in the Arab/Palestinian–Israeli theatre. A formal peace has been achieved between Israel and both Egypt and Jordan. But peace has proved elusive between Israel and the Palestinians, in spite of the optimism of the 1990s. With the current decade dominated by violence, future prospects for peace are as poor as they have been at any time since the late 1980s

The Middle East has experienced an arms race at various times since the 1950s. On occasion warfare has been industrial in its scale and impact, with the Iran–Iraq war the notable illustration. The devastation caused has been the product of the intensity of the firepower that has been marshalled by local states and the involvement of the world's remaining superpower, the

US, from outside. The US has become increasingly embroiled in regional conflict since 1990. Warfare has also been increasingly asymmetrical, which means that casualties have usually been largely one-sided. Non-state actors, notably various Kurdish and Palestinian communities, have been the most vulnerable. With many foundational issues still undecided, it remains a fair bet that conflict will continue to punctuate life in the region, especially along the Israeli rim and in the northern Gulf.

5

Development

The Third World is full of mono-cultural (single commodity dominated) economies, and the Middle East is no exception. However, the Middle East's situation is slightly different to those found in parts of sub-Saharan Africa or some of the island states in the Carribean. Instead of bananas, cocoa or rubber, the basis of the mono-culture, especially in the smaller economies of the Gulf, is hydrocarbons, namely oil and gas. Though one would probably feel more blessed to be the producer of crude oil rather than say palm oil, both are firmly located in the category of what economists have come to call the 'resource curse'. That is to say, single commodities the size and dominance of which have a grossly distorting effect on the overall national economy, and where an often volatile export price on the global markets brings instability in the budgeting and planning processes of those economies. It is no coincidence that the most successful economies in the Middle East, Israel and Turkey, have relatively diversified economies and are not dependent on the uncertainties of a single, dominant, primary commodity. Arguably, it is no coincidence that they have the most successfully functioning polities as well.

The oil mono-culture

It was an accident of geology that most of the Middle East's oil and gas reserves were found in the most underdeveloped parts of the region. This coincided primarily with the smaller Gulf states – the UAE (Abu Dhabi overwhelmingly its main producer member), Kuwait, Qatar and the somewhat larger Saudi Arabia in particular – together with Libya. Indeed until well into the 1950s so modest was the Libyan economy that its biggest export earner was scrap metal left over from the North Africa campaign of the Second World War. The economy of the newly created Kingdom of Saudi Arabia, today's largest regional oil producer having earned $233 billion in exports in 2007, was dominated by the annual pilgrimage, some marginal agriculture and trade. That all changed with the discovery of oil in the 1930s by Western oil companies.

Owing to their relative underdevelopment, the impact of oil production on these countries was profound, both economically and politically. The rapidly expanding economies were dominated by economic rents, defined as income derived from non-productive activities, rather than such traditional productive sectors as agriculture or industry. This meant that there was little by way of a conventional economy, capable of either generating complementary sources of wealth to oil or of providing employment for its nationals. Furthermore, the fact that these rents were generated abroad meant that there was only a modest additional boost to the national economy through the knock-on impact of such activities, the multiplier effect. Neither was there much of a trickle down in terms of skills transfers; in the capital intensive nature of the oil sector about the best that locals could expect during the early decades was to become drivers for the international oil companies.

Instead, the impact of oil rents had a distorting effect on the national economy. The absence of a significant range of goods and services produced at home meant that there were relatively few things that the new externally generated income could be spent on. Property quickly proved to be a rare focus, with its consequent inflationary effects upon land prices. The construction sector emerged as one of the few areas of the economy to benefit from a secondary impact of oil rents. This, however, tended to take the form of the building of large villas for members of the ruling regimes, and those enjoying their patronage. In the absence of vigorous and sustainable local production, the new oil earnings sucked in imports, creating large balance of trade deficits. It was the external economy rather than the national economy that satisfied the demand for such diverse goods as consumer durables, building materials and military materiel.

Oil also had a distorting effect on the convertibility of the national currencies of the new hydrocarbon economies through the phenomenon of 'Dutch Disease'. Because the Gulf states and Libya produced very little their national currencies should consequently have been worth little in the foreign exchange markets. This could have provided an opportunity for the development of an export oriented economy, because of the low costs of the factors of production (i.e. land, capital, labour) at home and hence the potentially competitive prices that they could charge on the international market. However, the export of oil created a single sector-oriented demand for the national currency as oil earnings, priced near universally in US dollars, were converted back. Relative to the productive sectors at home the national currency became extremely over-valued, thereby inflating local costs and potential export prices alike. Not surprisingly this diminished the prospects for foreign direct investment (FDI), here defined as long-term, inward investment from abroad. Such investment had already been largely put off by the small size of most of the oil producers' domestic markets, there simply being insufficient local demand for most locally produced manufactured goods. The term 'Dutch Disease' was coined from the predicament of the gas export market in Holland. If gas was a distorting factor in an advanced, diversified country like that of the Netherlands, it gives a sense of how much more distorting a dominant commodity like oil would be in a more modestly sized, mono-cultural economy in the Middle East.

No taxation, no representation

Because of the cock-eyed nature of wealth creation in the Gulf states and Libya, the relationship between state and society developed in an unfamiliar and counter-intuitive way. Giacomo Luciani has drawn attention to this in the distinction that he has made between production and allocation states. In the former, the conventional world experience, the state extracts income from the productive sectors of the economy in the form of the direct taxation that it levies from workers and companies. With this income the state funds activities for which it is generally agreed it is responsible, from external defence to the justice system at home to a range of domestic government services, including welfare provisions, education and health.

By contrast, in allocation states income is generated by flows accruing directly to the state exchequer in the form of oil rents. Society is consequently bypassed, both as the main locomotive of economic growth, and as the main source of state income. With no or little direct taxation required, the function of the state is therefore changed. Instead, of resource collector, the state plays the role of resource distributor within the system. This means that the state is not beholden to society but is elevated above it. As a consequence, the citizen is transformed into a supplicant, experiencing a one-way relationship with the state, as a job seeker or perhaps as the owner of a company chasing state contracts. The state, by contrast, enjoys relative autonomy from society. Theoretically at least the state does not have to be wary of society or pander to its special interests.

Though this approach, called rentier state theory, has remained the dominant one as far as the analysis of the Gulf states and Libya is concerned since the 1980s, it is not problem free. To this end a brief critique is in order.

- First, there has been some unease at the reductionism of the theory, which privileges oil rents as the key driver of both economic structure and behaviour, well ahead of all other factors. Even in such extreme, near-laboratory conditions as the Gulf states, there needs to be room to bring other tools of analysis to bear.

- Second, even a cursory look at the oil dominated economies of the region indicates that politics has not faded away, even in a context of abundant resources, as accrued during the oil bonanza years of the mid-1970s. The ideological politics of radical Islamism has remained in evidence, albeit at fluctuating levels of intensity throughout the period of super oil wealth, suggesting that ideas do matter.

- Third, one may also challenge the ideal typical portrayal of the state as having been cut free from its dependence on society. Evidence suggests that civil society has simply intensified its engagement with the state in order to gain access to the rising resource levels at its disposal, with the strategies of those seeking to penetrate the various branches of the state becoming more sophisticated or focused.

- Fourth, rentier state theory, while certainly conceptually illuminating, has its limitations of insight. What best explains the chaotic inefficiencies of the first oil boom of the 1970s, the structural impact of oil or the corrupt and self-serving agency of the region's leaders who were responsible for its management?

This is the point at which the rentier economies of the oil producing states, here understood to be economies characterised by the distorting effects of rents on them, begin to have a political impact. Because of the unsophistication of the early oil states, there was little sense of differentiation between state coffers and the regimes in power. Indeed, in countries like Abu Dhabi, Kuwait and Saudi Arabia, the senior royals also held the top positions of government. In the initial phase of oil sales, much of the income flowing into the state found its way into the personal possession of the ruling families and their cronies.

These flows gave regimes extensive powers of patronage and the ability to co-opt constituencies of potential political support, from tribes to businessmen. The new wealth was distributed selectively in the form, for example, of contracts and employment creation. Under-employment continues to be a chronic problem in the oil states. In Saudi ministries one can gauge the importance of a post holder by the number of well turned out flunkies that emerge to meet and greet visitors on the way to the office of the man in charge.

TRADITIONAL CHECKS

A good example of traditional checks and balances, and their demise, is Kuwait, where the Sabah family emerged as the administrators of the emirate in the eighteenth and nineteenth centuries, while the other major families of the day made money from trade. The merchant families exercised a restraining leverage over the Sabah through their role as principal taxpayers. The first sign of political aggrandisement could be snuffed out through the withholding of income. This fiscal-related balance at the centre was undermined when oil rents began to flow direct to the state. The Sabah had discovered an independent source of funds, and was therefore no longer dependent on the merchant families, as of old. Moreover, those funds were much greater in magnitude than any taxes that the commercial families could have afforded, transforming the economic and hence the political relationship in the emirate. Consequently, the merchants lost their leverage and became dependent on the political centre for economic benefits. An important source of political balance, which had emerged through local, culturally acceptable, dynamics and which had worked efficiently, had disappeared. Kuwait was, however, spared what might have been a more autocratic form of rule by the emergence of the beginnings of a representative institution, the National Assembly, in the 1930s, before the erosion of these traditional checks.

With so much patronage power at the disposal of the ruling families traditional checks and balances, the type of which exist within a predominantly tribal system, began to break down. The social hierarchy of power, traditionally rather flat, gave way to heightened deference to the political centre. A new social contract began implicitly to emerge: provided the rulers used the oil wealth to create a generous welfare state they would expect no demands from the general populace for a share in governance.

The historical progression of the oil markets

Prior to the 1970s, the international oil companies (IOC) had the upper hand in the relationship with the oil producing states, a reflection of the concentration of expertise among the IOCs, the dependent nature of the states themselves and the global context of colonialism in the region. Within this relationship the IOCs decided on the price of oil, and the oil producing states were the passive recipients of the income that accrued. As the volume of oil exports grew the ruling regimes did well from the relationship, but not as well as the IOCs. From the early 1960s the income was of such magnitude that using it exclusively for regime consumption and patronage was no longer sustainable. It began to be used for the general good in countries like Saudi Arabia. The acute imbalance in the relationship between oil states and oil companies remained.

This reality broke down between 1969 and 1973. The advent of regime change in Libya in September 1969 brought to power a free officers movement led by Mu'amar al-Qadhafi. He helped to erode the strong position occupied by the IOCs by ending the American and British military presence in Libya and insisting on renegotiating the oil fee structure. Buoyed by his success, Qadhafi's Libya went on to nationalise the foreign companies involved in exploration and production in May 1970. With the global economy of the day increasingly characterised by a 'mixed' experience under which the state had control of the commanding heights, other oil producing countries subsequently followed suit. This practice even spread to the likes of Kuwait and Saudi Arabia, hitherto firmly allied with the governments of the countries from which these IOCs came. So well established had this practice become that oil producing states could nationalise such companies without fear of a Mossadeq-type political challenge from the oil company's parent states.

If the oil company nationalisations of the early to mid-1970s provided a recalibrated relationship between producing states and IOCs, it was the massive oil hikes of 1973–74 that transformed crude oil into a high earning commodity. The trigger for this change came with the 1973 Arab–Israeli war and the use of crude oil by the region's largest producer, Saudi Arabia, as an instrument of diplomatic leverage. The actual move was relatively modest: oil sales to the US were cut, as they were by ten per cent to the Netherlands, the Dutch being Israel's main European backer. The market reaction was incendiary. Oil prices famously quadrupled. The impact on the consumers and their economies was immediate and profound. There were long queues at gas stations across the US. The capitalist economies of the West were plunged into recession. The collapse of the Western economies was only prevented by the recipients of the massive surge in oil rents recycling their new-found income back into a Western controlled financial system. It was the surge in deposits received by the banking sector that led to the search for new lending markets, the profligacy that ensued ultimately resulting in the Latin American debt crisis of the 1980s.

SAUDI OIL

Oil was discovered in Saudi Arabia in 1938 by the leading US oil companies of the day, popularly known as 'the Seven Sisters', which came together to form a consortium, the Arabian–American Oil Company (Aramco). As Britain dominated the oil industries of Iran, Iraq and the small Gulf states such as Kuwait, US companies concentrated on Saudi Arabia, and would be pre-eminent in the kingdom for nearly four decades. The main centre of the Saudi oil industry is al-Hasa, the Eastern Province, the region that is home to the kingdom's significant Shia minority (approximately forty per cent of the province, though just five per cent of the kingdom). Saudi Arabia's known oil reserves stand at around 100 billion barrels. Because of the magnitude of these reserves little active prospecting takes place in the kingdom, so the true level could be considerably higher. As well as having the world's highest country reserves, the cost of production in the kingdom is modest at around $1–$1.5/barrel, less than ten per cent of the equivalent recovery costs in the North Sea. With its high reserves and high production levels, normally between eight million and ten million b/d, Saudi Arabia has traditionally acted as an oil price dove. In contrast to the hawks like Iran and Algeria, who would rather maximise income through high production and high prices in the short term, the kingdom aims for the long-term stability of the oil market to ensure its own long-term prosperity. For oil in the ground is not the same as income in the bank; as a well-known oil sector aphorism has it, the Stone Age did not come to an end because the world ran out of stone.

Though the Saudis have repeatedly renounced the use of oil as a political weapon since 1973, and have largely been as good as their word, fear of energy price hikes have ever since preoccupied the minds of governments and market traders, ensuring sizeable risk premiums in the international traded price. Though international oil prices climbed dramatically in the mid-1970s they have been anything but consistent in their levels ever since.

The major landmarks of the international oil markets, illustrating the dominant impact of the Middle East, have been as follows:

- **Era of high prices, 1973–85**. Oil prices were volatile during this period, the post 1974 dip helping to precipitate the domestic unrest that resulted in the Iranian revolution of 1978–79. The revolution itself then triggered a further peak in prices, above the $40/barrel threshold, a high that was carried on once the Iran–Iraq War had broken out in September 1980, owing to the disruption of the oil supplies of both sides.
- **Price collapse, 1986**. With new, non-Opec production having been incentivised by high prices and supply disruptions, the oil price came under intense downward pressure in the early to mid-1980s. Notional cartel prices were only defended by Saudi Arabia acting as the 'swing producer', that is to say reducing output in order to maintain the supply-demand equation. By 1985, however, Saudi production had been cut by two-thirds to some 3.2 million b/d, an untenable level. With Riyadh also acting politically in order to put pressure on Iran to disable its war effort, the kingdom abandoned its swing role. Saudi supplies went back up and prices crashed.
- **Era of low prices, 1986–97**. Oil prices settled into the $16–$25 band, less than half the level of what had until then been the nominal price. With their control of the market, it was the Saudis who were most instrumental in the setting of this price. Its rationale was that in contrast to the 1970s, oil prices should be affordable, thereby guaranteeing a long-term market for the kingdom's massive oil reserves. The lower prices had unforeseen consequences elsewhere in the region, however. They put great pressure on those economies whose structure had been predicated on the reliability of significantly higher oil prices. Those countries that would as early

as 1988 hit the fiscal and political wall as a result of these lower oil prices included Algeria and Jordan.

- **Price spike, 1990**. A brief departure from the norm came in August 1990, when oil prices spiked above $40/barrel in response to the Iraqi invasion of Kuwait. The loss of Kuwaiti production owing to conflict and Iraqi production because of UN endorsed international sanctions appeared to preface a renewed bout of higher prices. However, Saudi Arabia raised its production levels from eight million b/d to ten million b/d, thereby making good the combined deficit. With world markets becalmed, prices fell back to the status quo ante and hardly moved again, in spite of the US-led liberatation of Kuwait in January and February 1991.

- **Opec miscalculation, 1997**. In an effort to nudge incomes higher, the Opec meeting in Jakarta in November 1997 raised the quotas of member states. It was a disastrous miscalculation regarding emerging trends in world oil demand, especially with the Asian financial crisis around the corner. The result was that prices plummeted as low as $10/barrel on the back of an excess of supply over demand. These basement level prices threatened the stability of a number of the larger producing states in the Middle East. The consequent meagre foreign exchange income was, for example, insufficient for Iran to cover even its essential civilian imports bill.

- **New era: oil price recovery.** Faced with economic and political catastrophe, Iran and Saudi Arabia, until recently sworn enemies across the Gulf, concluded a deal at The Hague in spring 1998 that returned upward momentum to the market. This agreement felicitously coincided with the stabilisation of bilateral relations, thereby underpinning the oil deal. The oil price temporarily stabilised in the $22–$28 b/d band, the preferred Saudi range. However, the growing expectation of a US invasion of Iraq applied further upward pressure on prices. The weakness of the dollar, a shortage of world refining capacity and low oil price driven long neglected investment in upstream oil since the mid-1980s maintained market tightness. Crucially, Riyadh appeared to drop its opposition to prices above $40–$50/barrel, angry at the taxes being heaped on retail energy prices by Western consumer governments. By the beginning of 2008 the international oil price had topped the $100/barrel level, comparable to the real value of mid-1970s' oil prices.

* **Global recession and a price rout.** With fears of a global depression, the consequence of the credit crunch, oil prices began to tumble from the August 2008 high of over $145/b to less than $50/b at the end of that year. Riyadh appears currently to favour prices of $75/b. Successive, hurried Opec meetings aimed at reining in supply proved to be too little too late. The year 2008 once again underlined the difficulty of macro-economic management in the oil producing countries owing to the instability of their mono-cultures. In the short to medium terms, the likes of Abu Dhabi and Saudi Arabia have probably stacked sufficient financial resources to ride the period of low prices. Iran, with its much larger population, and more profligate political leadership, is much more vulnerable. Yet, few of those connected with the oil business are unduly pessimistic about the medium to long term. An end to depression will trigger increased global energy use. With the absence of investment accentuating the factors that stoked price growth to $145/b, a sudden and equally volatile return to exorbitant oil prices may confidently be predicted over the medium to long term.

The regional economy

Hitherto the discussion has focused on the hydrocarbon producing countries and in particular the small states of the Gulf. Does this then mean that the region can best be divided into two: oil rich, rentier political economies on the one hand; oil poor, cash poor states on the other? The simple answer is that this dichotomy did indeed catch something of the economic and social polarisation of the region in the 1970s. At that time agriculture was still an important sector. Patches of industrialisation had grown up in the region, notably in Egypt. Since then a number of mechanisms have emerged through which oil generated income has been recycled across the region, producing rentier characteristics, even in many of the non-hydrocarbons

Table 1 Per capita income of oil producing and non-oil producing countries, 2008

Country	Per capita income (US $)	World rank
Algeria	6,500	98
Bahrain	32,100	28
Egypt	5,500	102
Iraq	3,600	129
Iran	10,600	75
Israel	25,800	36
Jordan	4,900	112
Kuwait	39,300	11
Lebanon	11,300	70
Libya	12,300	65
Morocco	4,100	121
Oman	24,000	41
Qatar	80,900	1
Saudi Arabia	23,200	42
Sudan	2,200	145
Syria	4,500	119
Tunisia	7,500	92
Turkey	12,900	63
UAE	37,300	18
Yemen	2,300	144

Source: CIA, *The World Factbook.*

states. Consequently, from the 1980s onwards some of these extremities of wealth have been softened, even if there remains a broad reality that the smaller oil producing countries enjoy greater wealth than their non-hydrocarbons counterparts. These extremities of wealth reappeared with the dramatic resurgence of oil prices in the mid-2000s.

Up to the 1970s the Middle East regional economy was one where agriculture still dominated, much of it subsistence in orientation. As late as the 1980s it was still fashionable to refer to the likes of Iraq and Sudan as 'the breadbasket' of the Middle East, even though output was depressed, and, in the case of the former, soil salination levels were increasing. The rural population still outstripped the urban. Levels of illiteracy, especially among rurally based women, were still high.

This reality changed with the advent of oil rents, whereby the newly enriched states acted as a labour magnet for the region. This phenomenon began in the 1950s, as rising income accrued to the smaller Gulf states. These entities did not have the skilled labour force necessary to man the new positions being created in the public sector as a result of oil. Instead, these states looked elsewhere in the region for workers, because they spoke the same language and had similar cultural, especially religious, backgrounds. Large numbers of Palestinians, relatively well educated and looking for new opportunities after the experiences of conflict and dispersal, moved to countries like Kuwait and Saudi Arabia, where they worked in the white collar professions. By the end of the 1980s some 400,000 of Kuwait's total population of two million were Palestinian. They were followed by Egyptian migrants, who worked in the professions, as accountants and teachers, especially in the newly expanding education sector in the Gulf.

This steady regional trend turned into a wave with the onset of super oil rents in the 1970s. Large numbers of rural Egyptians moved to the Gulf and Iraq to work in agriculture and construction, both because of the labour shortage and the perceived ignobility of blue collar work on the part of the more effete Gulf Arabs. Even relatively well-educated Egyptians accepted menial jobs abroad because of the great differential in earnings. They were followed by successive waves of Jordanians, Palestinians and Syrians. It was Tunisian labour that primarily filled the new posts opening up in Libya. For many of the latter migrants their families remained at home, the recipients of the new wealth sent back by their predominantly male family members abroad. A new generation of consumers emerged in the villages of upper Egypt, with white goods and audio-visual products previously undreamt of now within the grasp of hitherto poor, rural families.

Though this labour migration carried risks for the exporting countries, notably in the form of a brain drain, the consequent levels of remittances helped in other ways, for instance in alleviating the pressure on the balance of payments. This unwisely tempted political leaders to celebrate the surge in demographic growth, resulting from the baby boom of the 1970s. Two decades later and with unemployment casting a regional shadow, the Middle East's population and what to do with it had turned into a serious challenge.

Remittances were not the only device through which income levels were spread across the region. Those states flush with oil cash set about using their new-found wealth as an instrument of political influence. The elites of the poorer parts of the region, from the heads of state through members of the political elite, to opposition figures and even some professions like journalists, were the recipients of cash or benefits in kind. When he swept into town for the 1980 Arab summit in Amman, Jordan, the Iraqi leader, Saddam Hussein arrived with a fleet of more than fifty top of the range Mercedes cars, ready to dispense as gifts to favoured members of the Jordanian media. This was assumed to be merely the tip of a very large iceberg.

The high point of state to state Arab aid came with the major Arab summits held in Baghdad in 1987 and 1988. In a bid to dissuade Israel's Arab neighbours from joining Egypt in its separate peace deal, a ten-year aid commitment was announced worth nearly $3 billion a year. Though only honoured up to one-third of the pledge, as oil prices slid, the grand nature of the commitment gives a sense of the virility of the petro-diplomacy of the age and the political dependencies that it engendered, especially among the non-oil states.

Finally, many of the oil rich states established or patronised multilateral mechanisms for aiding the less well off states of the region and indeed beyond. Such activities enhanced the prestige of the donor countries, as well as enabling them to claim that they were honouring the Islamic invocation towards alms giving. Major organisations that distributed development funds, both in the Middle East and the wider developing world, included:

- the Kuwait Fund for Arab Economic Development (est. 1961), which comfortably exceeds the UN international aid target of 0.7% of GDP;
- the Arab Fund for Economic and Social Development (est. 1972), an Arab League organisation, also Kuwait based;
- the Abu Dhabi Fund for Development (est. 1971);
- the Saudi Fund for Development (est. 1975).

The effectiveness of the strategy for increasing international leverage was thrown into doubt following the Iraqi invasion of Kuwait. In 1990 Kuwait discovered how little popular support had been generated by such handouts, as it sought to rally public opinion, both in the Arab world and beyond. In much of North Africa, in particular, governments, in spite of their better instincts, were obliged to temper their support for the victim of the invasion under public pressure at home. In the aftermath of the liberation, Kuwait determined to change the way in which its aid was distributed in the future, with a view to establishing direct relations with sectoral and project beneficiaries.

It was not through aid and transfers alone that the disparities in wealth were partially ameliorated. The oil bonanza of the 1970s stimulated much exploration across the region and beyond. Though oil and gas finds paled in comparison with the Gulf, primary energy output ('upstream' production) proved to be a useful source of foreign exchange for a number of the poorer economies. Even oil production under 500,000 b/d provided a significant foreign exchange and fiscal boost in poorer countries like Syria and Yemen. While Egypt had little oil, it did discover significant levels of gas. Though prices and margins are more modest than with oil, gas production also helped the exchequer as it grappled with unfavourable external conditions. Algeria has found even larger deposits of natural gas in its desert interior, thereby taking the slack of an oil industry that is steadily diminishing in output. The cleaner nature of gas has the added bonus of being more environmentally friendly and hence a more sustainable source of energy exports long term.

Contrasting development strategies

The prevalence of oil rents in the regional political economy has thrown down a challenge to the development planners of the states of the region. The range of responses illustrates the differing constraints and opportunities available. They also indicate just how far from conventional economics many of the states of the Middle East now find themselves. Five examples will illustrate the situation.

1. **Algeria: corruption not catch-up.** When Algeria became independent it was ambitious and in a hurry: it was a non-

aligned country that wanted to lead the developing world. The economic aspect of this strategy was to reduce the level of dependency on a withering oil sector by establishing a strong productive economy. The state was given a privileged position in this strategy, partly because of the small size of the private sector and partly because of the fashion in the 1960s for state socialism. However, things soon went wrong. First, Algeria backed heavy industrial investment, just as the sector moved towards obsolescence. Second, rampant state corruption displaced purely economic calculations in decision-making. Third, protectionism at home resulted in gross inefficiencies. Rather than diversifying the economy, Algeria became more dependent on its oil and subsequently its gas sectors.

2. **Saudi Arabia: the wrong sort of strengths.** Apart from some heavily protected crony capitalism, Saudi Arabia had no industrial sector to speak of in the 1970s. Riyadh began to diversify in the 1980s based on the sound reasoning of comparative advantage, that is to say make what you are good at and can do better or more cheaply than your rivals. An oil refining industrial sector based on plastics and chemicals emerged ('downstream' development), taking advantage of the country's cheap and proximate energy inputs. These were mostly forged in joint ventures with various multinational companies (MNCs), from India and Japan as well as Europe and the US. The MNCs brought specialist expertise, quality control, and even guaranteed foreign markets to the table. These investments in places like the industrial cities of Jubail on the Gulf shore and Yanbu on the Red Sea have been great successes, generating steady profits and export earnings. Successful though it has undoubtedly been, it has proved to be the wrong sort of comparative advantage. With a burgeoning population, it is labour intensive investment success that Saudi Arabia craves, rather than capital intensive

industries. The latter have done little to soak up the country's increasingly problematic unemployed, leading to long-term concerns about stability.

3. **Kuwait: throwing away the economics textbook.** There was no model for Kuwaiti economic development in the 1970s/80s. The country's domestic market was too small; its inhospitable ecology too difficult for agriculture and industry. Instead, development planners threw away their economic textbooks. They sent the capital accruing through oil sales offshore in a portfolio of diversified investments, spanning property, stocks and shares, and direct company investment. The creation of a parallel reserve, entitled piously 'The Fund for Future Generations', was established to ensure that the country enjoyed the proceeds of oil in perpetuity. By the end of the 1980s the strategy had been vindicated: the emirate was earning as much from its foreign portfolio as it was from its total crude oil exports. Further vindication came with the 1990 Iraqi invasion, The Iraqis dismantled and repatriated most of Kuwait's movable assets (that which they did not destroy). Large accumulated fixed asset investments at home would have been smashed or stolen. Much of the reserves had to be run down to fund the liberation of Kuwait, together with reconstruction, though they have been built back up in part since.

4. **Tunisia: looking to Europe.** If the Arab world is made up of heavily distorted economies, Tunisia's is the one that elicits most hope. It does so because it is not burdened with resource curse. To its credit, it is the one Arab country that has kept control of the birth rate, through a progressive health strategy, which has included dedicated advanced provision for women. Unlike the nonsense heard of elsewhere in the region, it has regarded population growth as neither a gift from God nor as a prized asset. If a significant proportion of Tunisia's wealth came from Libya in the past, Europe is becoming the centre

of its economic gravity today. The tourist industry has been developed with the mid-range European market in mind. Agricultural produce is exported northwards. Together with Morocco, Tunisia is at the forefront of Arab economic reform, with European influence and opportunities in mind. If it was not for the fact that the country has one of the most crudely authoritarian and self-serving regimes in the region, its economic prospects might even be sanguine.

5. **Dubai: brand development.** Dubai's economic development has been powered by two considerations: oil production that is all but spent; a dogged desire not to be dominated by its local rival, oil abundant Abu Dhabi. For more than three decades Dubai has thought creatively about how to address the former and hence achieve the latter. It has done so by monetarising the laissez-faire atmosphere that exists in the emirate, embracing a cosmopolitan existence and boldly initiating 'wow factor' investments. The re-export trade, exploiting its natural harbour, has always been a strength of Dubai, which has played a major role in sanctions busting Iran and Iraq since the 1980s. It has built on this strength by making itself into the Gulf's most attractive regional centre, with service sector strengths as diverse as conferences, tourism and maritime repairs. Since the 1980s Dubai has worked hard at enhancing a quality brand, which is well illustrated by its luxury property and hotel sector portfolios, epitomised by its palm development and the world's only seven star rating respectively. Though initially a resounding success, there has been a fragility about Dubai's achievements that has given it a feeling of a bubble. The effects of the global financial crisis in 2008 – falling property prices, ailing property companies and difficulties at Dubai's Emirates airlines – have plunged Dubai into a period of acute uncertainty, and, almost as bad from its perspective, a renewed dependency on Abu Dhabi.

The regional outliers

This section began by noting the economic success of Israel and Turkey, relative to the other main states of the Middle East. That does not mean that both have been immune to the rentierism that has affected the region. Israel has been a frequent recipient of income arriving from outside its borders. Most obviously, Israel has been the largest single country recipient of bilateral aid from the US. Turkey too was the routine recipient of military aid, especially from the US and Germany, until the end of the Cold War. Nevertheless, the take-off in the productive and service economies of both countries since the 1990s has ensured that the foreign exchange earnings in the form of rents have been a rapidly diminishing proportion of the whole.

The Turkish economy was for a long time prior to the 1970s virtually self-sufficient, a product of its large agriculture sector. Business was inward looking. Economic policy was focused on import substitution, a strategy of trying to replace imports by making them at home typical of the developing world in the 1960s/70s. By contrast, little was made for export. This economic comfort zone became unsustainable as a result of the large increases in the oil price, which hit Turkey hard as an energy import dependent country. In the late 1970s Turkey struggled to cope, being hit from both ends, with partial electricity blackouts coexisting with a spiralling foreign debt needed to afford even limited volumes of energy.

This vicious cycle was only snapped by the 1980 coup and the emergence of Turgut Ozal, as the junta's economic policy supremo. He transformed the nature of the Turkish economy into one firmly oriented towards exports. The newly invigorated and less state dependent private sector in Turkey took full advantage of the collapse of Communism to enter the new economies of the former Soviet Union, with gas proving to be the motor of trade in the other direction.

Exports also took off to Europe, particularly in textiles, as the expanding EU increasingly emerged as the centre of economic gravity for Turkey. In 1996 Turkey and the EU created a Customs Union, designed to integrate their economies, especially in the field of manufacturing. This created the backdrop for the 1999 decision to make Turkey a candidate member of the Union. In 2004 accession negotiations began. While they have been erratic to date, and there are many bilateral obstacles to full membership, there is no comparable alternative. Since 2004, as Turkey's EU perspective has sharpened, so foreign direct investment (FDI) has picked up. It grew from a disappointing $0.5 billion a year since the 1980s to the $21.9 billion mark in 2007. With investments as diverse as Toyota and Vodaphone, Turkish prosperity has been growing rapidly.

As with most emerging markets, however, the Turkish economy has its vulnerabilities. Its annual rate of seven per cent real growth has been achieved during the 2000s more under the stewardship of the IMF than the leadership of its own governments. The Fund was called in (for the seventeenth time in Turkey's history) after successive financial crises in 2000 and 2001, when political problems precipitated unsettling financial turbulence. That in turn had been triggered by instability in the Turkish banking system, and an unhealthy insider relationship between some of the political parties and the country's state banks. For a moment, Turkey's situation was worse than Argentina's. Though much of this crony capitalism has now been cleaned out, Turkey remains susceptible to the chief complaints of emerging markets, especially at a time of a global credit crunch: loss of investment confidence; risk aversion in the financial markets; exchange rate fluctuations; inflation; debt management problems; recession, and consequent social problems (mindful of the young population) if growth comes to a juddering halt. While the commercialisation of the Turkish economy has made impressive leaps forward since the mid-

1990s, and the long-term growth expectations (e.g. judged by the consumer goods lag in comparison with the EU) are good, shorter run stop-go experiences cannot be ruled out.

Israel went through its own economic epiphany at about the same time as Turkey. In Israel's case, hyperinflation, a dependent state sector and a powerful trade union movement created a context in which there was widespread agreement that neo-liberal economic reform was necessary. The outcome was economic transformation that virtually paralleled Reaganomics and Thatcherism. Extensive privatisation, the rapid emergence of hi-tech and private security sectors, the integration of the Tel Aviv stock exchange into the international portfolio investment market all followed to transform the country's economic landscape. With inflation and the unions beaten, the dominant game in Israel is an individualist, entrepreneurial one.

In the 1990s, much interest in Israel was based on the assumption that a historic settlement to the Arab/Palestinian–Israel conflict was a done deal. Optimistic ideas, such as Shimon Peres's 'New Middle East', in which he foresaw a prosperous and economically integrated space embracing Israel, the Palestinians and Jordan, proved to be premature to say the least. When the second Palestinian uprising broke out, with its suicide bombings, Israel tipped into a deep recession. Its unemployment rate of eleven per cent was the worst in the country's history. The re-establishment of security, in part through the construction of a security barrier, helped to restore confidence. Israel's swingeing economic reforms of the early 2000s have provided a firm foundation for the return to a recognisably Western-style growth in the middle of the decade. However, Israel's increasing integration into the world economy also makes it vulnerable to global depression, and all of the profound uncertainties associated with it.

Much of the Middle East has risen without trace as far as the goals of economic and social development are concerned. The capital cities of the high wealth states in the region enjoy many of the medals of success: multi-lane highways; grandiose buildings of steel and glass; fancy shopping malls, full of American franchises. But do they deserve them? The roots of such success are shallow, the product of oil wealth and the regional circulation of such income, rather than the sustained success of well anchored, productive economic activity. A litany of factors are responsible for the latter: the distorting nature of oil rents; the clumsy nature of state economic control; rampant corruption among the political class; no clear strategy for economic growth. Only selectively – in the resourcefulness of Iraqi engineers, the vigour of the Turkish textile trade, the competence of the local oil production staff at Saudi Aramco, and the canniness of much of the region's merchant class – has real success been achieved. The Middle East is modern rather than developed. Extremes of income exist, both within states, and across the region. In the growing region-wide challenges of unemployment, low grade labour and an education system struggling to produce quality as well as quantity, the region will face its greatest challenges.

6
Governance

The vast majority of the states of the Middle East have struggled with the concept of good governance – accountable executives, party pluralism, participatory politics, personal freedoms and human rights – since their emergence as independent entities. In formal terms their positions are not at all bad. Rhetorically, the region has signed up to many of the various international conventions, for instance on human rights. Practically, one may find the periodic holding of elections and the existence of elected assemblies. Some countries, such as Jordan and Morocco, have multiple political parties. In spite of these trappings of participatory government the actual record of states on the global good governance agenda is a contrasting one. There has been a real failure to internalise and operationalise the values of good governance listed above. In the region, only Israel (though not without its own shortcomings) and to a degree Turkey can be described as substantive democracies. While some states have taken varying and largely tentative steps in the direction of political reform, the performance of Libya, Syria and Sudan is as bad as one might find anywhere in the most repressive parts of the world.

A thin record on reform

Under the Ottomans, the notion of citizenship was a poorly developed concept. The ethos underpinning political relationships was that the individual should serve the state, rather than the other way around, the basis of the modern European state.

The Ottoman state required two things from its subjects: army service and taxes. Other than in such extractive activities, individuals did not come into much contact with the Ottoman state. Even during the height of its reformist profile state–subject relations were limited. The main parts of the nineteenth-century reform strategy (*Tanzimat*) were directed at modernising the central bureaucracy, not state–society relations. During the moments of representative politics those taking part in the brief Ottoman experiment were confined to men of high birth.

It is therefore unsurprising that it was the patricians of the day from whom the leading figures of the European colonial period were drawn. In places like the Gulf states these leadership figures were members of an existing governing elite, entrenched since the eighteenth century and with their authority hardened through the possession of princely titles (kingship being frowned upon by some in the Muslim world). In the central lands of the Arab world, these patrician figures were predominantly landowners. These emerged as the main political figures of the 1920s and 1930s in the likes of Egypt and Syria. Another form of this 'politics of the notables' were the political figures grafted on to the newly created entities of the day, predominantly the Hashemites, who oversaw government in partnership with the British in Iraq and Transjordan.

The great dividing line in terms of political systems came during the regional political upheavals between 1949 and 1969. On the one hand, traditional, conservative forms of governance continued, predominantly in the Gulf, but also in conservative outposts like Jordan. These statelets were increasingly buffeted by the waves of radical politics, but through a combination of scale, the responsiveness of the political centre, and established and well understood political practice, domestic disaffection was kept in check. In these states population size was mainly small. Political processes were fluid and informal. The rulers in charge conducted political relationships in a highly personalised way, inviting individual petitions for specific benefits, such as seeking a job or money to treat a sick relative, rather than through structural reform or policy development. Thus, such benefits bestowed upon the individual were perceived as largesse from the ruler rather than from the state. Such actions bound individuals into a relationship of personal loyalty to the ruler. Good for the ruler, such a paternalistic approach did not help with the more abstract notions of state or nation building.

Standing in contrast to this conservative rim were the central states of the region, such as Egypt, Iraq, Syria and Algeria. These were the countries that had broken decisively with the old order, even if they had been less clear about their vision for its replacement. So, one of the first acts of the Free Officers in Cairo was to seize and break up the large holdings of the major landowners, who had dominated national politics together with the British and the palace during the inter-war years. In doing so, the Egyptian Free Officers ensured that there could be no political comeback by the old guard regime. In Algeria, all of the estimated one million French settlers had departed by independence. This was also the case with their Italian equivalents after the Qadhafi coup in Libya in 1969. Syria too saw nationalisations of what passed for the commanding heights of the economy in the early 1960s. Land seizures and nationalisations also followed the Ba'thist coup in Iraq in 1968.

While the radical regimes of the region began their lives with something of a reformist agenda, and based their legitimacy to rule on a transformatory ideology, it was not long before such sentiments had been forgotten. The radical officers and civilians of the 1950s and 1960s quickly morphed into an elite 'for itself', more broadly reminiscent, once stripped of the nominally militant slogans, of the more traditional elite for itself in the conservative states. Revelations by a former prime minister, Abdul Hamid Brahimi, in the late 1980s that the Algerian foreign debt of around $25 billion was the equivalent of the funds siphoned out of the system by the ruling elite over the previous two decades for their own profit had a totally believable symmetry to it.

There were other ways that the conduct of the radical elites in power were initially at least qualitatively different to that of the conservative elites during this time. While the latter used the selective distribution of benefits to a small and receptive population to underpin the traditional legitimacy of their rule, the former were not so fortunate. They had turned their backs on traditional forms of co-option, while the size and complexity of their polities rendered a comprehensive approach to inclusivity unfeasible. Though more representative than the old elites of the rising social structures of the day, the new ruling elites had to be careful in co-opting the co-members of their class for fear of promoting rivals who might one day become usurpers. Instead, they fell back on two devices to entrench their position in power. One, the growing rhetoric of radical transformation, whether it be in relation to the Arab–Israeli conflict, in the geopolitics of which they were intimately involved, or of socioeconomic transformation. Two, the brute force of repression.

The growth of the authoritarian state came to define milieu Arab politics between the 1960s and the 1980s. It consisted of both structure and ethos. The structural aspect involved the construction of a multiplicity of praetorian military units alongside a shadowy set of security bodies. The ethos behind such an initiative was to ensure that the military could no longer seize power as it had once done in the aftermath of independence through deploying relatively small numbers of men and equipment to seize a handful of strategic locations, such as the presidential palace and the radio station. The aim of the former was to have a well-armed and resourced military that could be called upon at a moment's notice to protect the regime and its senior figures. The creation by Rifaat al-Asad, the Syrian leader's brother, of an elite group called the 'Pink Panthers', so known because of the colour of their battle fatigues, was an eye-catching example in the 1980s. The creation of an elaborate security network, evocative of Orwell's *1984* in its conception and execution, was precisely designed to discourage plotting from within the elite for fear of the inevitability of discovery.

A VISIT TO THE INTELLIGENCE

A job offer in the public sector for a national, or a foreigner trying to obtain a residence permit would normally necessitate a visit to the General Intelligence Department/GID (*mukhabarat*), the most important and pervasive of security networks in most Arab countries. The appropriate approval would only be forthcoming once the GID had carried out an interview and checked to ensure that the individual was not guilty of undesirable political behaviour. Approval was usually received, but there was no guarantee, and there was certainly no right of appeal. Foreigners deemed to be undesirable could be deported without explanation or hesitation. The *mukhabarat* would actively pursue those nationals with a dissident background. In many Arab countries their tactics were similar to those used by the KGB in the USSR. Passports were seized, with foreign travel opportunities consequently curtailed; redundancy from public sector jobs could easily be engineered, jeopardising livelihood; individuals were often brought in for questioning for a few days duration, keeping up the pressure on individuals and families, and indicating to friends and neighbours that they should steer well clear; if needs be torture too could be used, especially at times of political tension and uncertainty. The threat of coercion was rarely hidden but was integrated as part of the overall system of political control. In pro-Western Jordan, the large and imposing GID headquarters was located at the confluence of four main roads close to central Amman until the 1990s; in Bahrain, everyone knew that the head of the Special Branch, responsible for internal security, was until the mid-1990s a Scot, Ian Henderson, a veteran of the counter-insurgency against the Mau Mau in Kenya before independence, and employed directly by the authorities in Manama.

The exceptions to the regional rules were to be found in Israel and Turkey. Israel had been established as an electoral democracy in 1948, drawing on the philosophical roots of the Jewish diaspora in Europe and the practices of its increasingly effective informal self-government in Palestine (*Yishuv*). The highly responsive nature of its single constituency parliamentary system, a Liberal Democrat's utopia, reflected a desire on the part of Israel's founding fathers to include the diverse backgrounds and values of the country's new citizenry. Though themselves secular in orientation, the founding generation of labour Zionists deliberately avoided the adoption of a written constitution for fear that it might have to clarify the relationship between religion and the state, and hence risk alienating the country's ultra-Orthodox Jews. Though based upon the erroneous secularist presumption that such a group would eventually fade away, eroded by the new values of modernity, it established the ground rules that would ensure Israel's status as a functioning democracy.

The ending of a range of security measures in the mainly Arab populated areas of Israel in the mid-1960s removed the main impediment to Israel's non-Jewish minority participation in national democratic politics. An attempt to co-opt the Arab vote using incentives faded over time, to be replaced by more politicised, nationalist parties. Concerns persist about the inclusivity of the Israeli system, mindful of the country's twenty per cent Arab population (not to be confused with the Palestinians resident in the occupied territories of the Gaza Strip and the West Bank), leading some commentators to describe the Israeli system as an 'ethnic democracy'. Nevertheless, the international benchmark of good governance, Freedom House, routinely labels Israel the only country that is unequivocally 'Free' in the Middle East region.

In Turkey, the journey towards participatory, representative politics began in 1946, with the ending of one party rule. In

1950 the incumbent government of the Republican People's Party relinquished power as a result of a general election, an early proof of a commitment to electoral politics. A set of internal and external considerations drove these reforms. The former related to the growing unpopularity of the regime because of the economic hardships sustained during the Second World War, in which the country was a non-combatant, but was deeply affected by the overall economic impact of war. The latter was the implied conditionality of a Western-style government if Turkey was to be admitted to such multilateral organisations as the Council of Europe and Nato. At the centre of both reasons was the threat from Soviet expansionism under Stalin, which threatened first invasion and then subversion.

The road towards democratic consolidation in Turkey has never been linear. Military interventions have taken place directly (in 1960 and 1980) and indirectly (in 1971 and 1997). In the 1970s, a vicious form of ideological politics spilled out onto the streets in the form of regular gun battles. In the early to mid-1990s, a number of shadowy gangs operated under the patronage of an opaque 'deep state' (*derin devlet*), the outcome including extra-judicial assassinations of Kurdish nationalists and other activists. Echoes of this 'dirty war' in Turkey were felt in 2008–9, with the Ergenekon revelations about the existence of a similar such gang. But neither has democratic politics been thoroughly compromised. Government has always been handed back to civilians after these interventions, even if the military enjoyed wide-ranging abilities to influence policy from behind the scenes. In the 1990s democratic consolidation from below began to catch up with the directed reform from above which had preceded it by more than three decades, notably in the beginnings of the creation of an independent civil society. In spite of these reforms it was possible up to 2002, and the election of the incumbent soft Islamist government, to label Turkey an electoral semi-authoritarian state.

Limited reform from above

The pressures for political reform in the Middle East began to build up from the late 1980s onwards. There were two main reasons for this. First, the impact of a shrinking aggregate regional economy on the back of the collapse of the world oil price in 1986. Those states that were most exposed, either because they did not have hydrocarbons and lived partly on handouts (e.g. Jordan) or had modest oil reserves and significantly larger populations (e.g. Algeria) were the first to get into serious trouble. In Jordan, currency collapse in 1988 and debt rescheduling in 1989 necessitated the adoption of a stringent IMF programme. The poor handling of consequent price rises led to riots in traditional East Bank areas, the bedrock of the regime, in April 1989; parliamentary elections were offered as a palliative for the strong economic medicine. In Algeria widespread riots in October 1988 resulted in the killing of hundreds of demonstrators by the army, only the subsequent offer of a liberal constitution and pluralist competitive politics succeeding in assuaging popular anger.

The impact of the contraction in oil rents would move centre stage in the mid-1990s, as the larger oil producing states of the region, notably Saudi Arabia and Iran, began to feel the fiscal pinch. Riyadh had been living beyond its means in deficit financing for most of the 1980s, complacent in the knowledge that sufficient reserves existed to make this a tenable medium-term strategy. The contingency cost of funding the US-led international coalition to eject Iraq from Kuwait rapidly accelerated this depletion, leaving government finances stretched and campaigns from Islamists and liberals alike for good governance reform. Forced to make cuts in spending and raise the price of utilities and telecoms, King Fahd responded by announcing a reform package that included a de facto constitution and the creation of a consultative council (*majlis al-shura*).

In the case of Iran it was 1998, the year of $10/barrel oil, when the exchequer hard landed, being unable to import its most basic needs. Fortunately for the regime in Tehran, a reform minded cleric, Mohammed Khatami, had been elected president in 1997. The hardliners in the regime let Khatami have latitude over popular reforms, such as the women's dress code, cultural freedoms and press pluralism. These sufficed to assuage the discontent of the majority of the people who had voted for Khatami until the oil price recovered and the hardliners were able to roll back some of Khatami's reforms, especially on press freedom.

SAUDI POLITICAL REFORM

Even by the standards of a reform-averse part of the world, Saudi Arabia was noteworthy for its absence of political reforms prior to 1993. If Kuwait was routinely regarded as the most liberal of the Gulf states, Saudi Arabia was indisputably the least. The other Gulf states shuffled between these two book-ends of the political continuum, with the relative size and wealth of the kingdom a deadweight on the cause of reform. Under King Abdul Aziz, the founder of the Saudi state, there had been an appointed consultative council (*majlis al-shura*), but even this institution had been lost over time. Reforms promised in 1962 had not materialised. This institutionally desertified state began to bloom in 1993, under pressure from both liberal and Islamist opinion in the kingdom. Fearing the effects of falling living standards and an embarrassing reliance on the US to protect the seat of Islam in 1990–91, King Fahd was effectively hussled into change. He consequently announced an Organic Law (comparable to a constitution), a law on succession and a law to establish consultative councils at the centre, and in the provinces of the kingdom. Though Fahd was fearful of change, the reforms were a quiet success, especially in promoting government responsiveness at a sub-national level. The Shura Council has expanded under Fahd's successor, King

> ### SAUDI POLITICAL REFORM (*cont.*)
>
> Abdullah, and has assumed a subsidiary committee structure comparable to a parliament. Ground-breaking change continues to progress tentatively, however. Cabinet reshuffles take place more frequently than in the past, but affect commoner rather than princely ministers. A shake-up of the senior members of the bureaucracy has so far proved to be an exception. The kingdom took its first step in the direction of electoral politics, with a small number of the seats on the capital's municipal council being filled through the polls in 2005. Women had their first experience as candidates and voters in the state endorsed elections for the Jeddah Chamber of Commerce later on in the year. Even an undoubted reformer like King Abdullah has been wary of too ready a resort to elections. In the ultra-conservative society that is the kingdom, Islamist and tribal candidates would be most likely to prosper in the event of the introduction of a responsive electoral system, with Western trained liberals sinking without trace. This argument has frequently been applied when Western governments have urged further domestic reform on the kingdom, an argument that has generally proved to be effective in lessening such external pressures.

The second reason for the increasing impetus behind political reform was the 'demonstration effect' of the collapse of the Soviet empire and the emergence of a collection of liberalising states in the developing world, including many of those on the continents of Latin America and sub-Saharan Africa. This factor has to be treated with care. Some of the loosening up of the Middle Eastern states (e.g. Algeria and Jordan mentioned above) had occurred before the positive domino effect of regime collapse in Eastern Europe. Also some of these changes, such as the fall of President Nicolae Ceacescu in Romania, were used by authoritarian regimes, notably that of Saddam Hussein in Iraq, to bind the ruling group more closely together.

Nevertheless, these changes were important because they brought home to presidents and emirs alike in the Middle East the emerging global momentum for liberal change. It was no longer acceptable for the Middle East to remain impervious to such influences.

The nature of the challenge to Middle East rulers had therefore changed. From the relatively straightforward retention of regime power emerged the altogether more ticklish goal of retaining power while implementing, or at least appearing to implement, reform. This was especially important because of the increasing need to mollify the US, the world's remaining superpower in an initially unipolar world in the aftermath of the Cold War. The US, as a government and as a society, was increasingly minded to use a range of liberal freedoms as a benchmark of how suitable the maintenance of cordial bilateral relations might be. This began with women's rights campaigners in the aftermath of the liberation of Kuwait, where women did not have the franchise, and continued with a gamut of freedoms. Unfortunately, Washington was easily satisfied as far as liberalisation and democratisation were concerned. The formal aspects of democracy, such as elections and assemblies, were increasingly confused with its substance, such as accountability, scrutiny and participation. This gave rulers and regimes a margin within which to operate. Thus was begun the era of limited reform from above.

An early proponent of this strategy was King Hussein of Jordan. He had no choice but to adopt substantive liberal reform because of the economic crisis of 1988–89. In addition to restoring an invigorated parliamentary life, political prisoners were released, political parties were legalised for the first time in three decades and press freedom flourished. In all of these areas the king was running to catch up with a pent-up will for reform. The situation changed in 1990–91 when, with corruption investigations pending, the king adroitly moved to maximise the opportunity for domestic benefits from the Iraq/Kuwait crisis. He indulged the pro-Saddam populism of his people and bought a new surge of instant popularity, albeit it at the cost of a passing criticism from among traditional friends in the West. In the intensity of the conflict and Hussein's newly galvanised popularity, corruption investigations, which it had been feared would go to the top, were quietly dropped. This renewed authority enabled the king to reposition himself at the forefront of the reform process.

Hussein subsequently proved able to throttle-back on liberal reforms once he had decided to make peace with Israel in 1994, for fear that these new liberal instruments could be used to target peace-making. The understanding that the king offered the political opposition in Jordan was that he would not force them to embrace the new peace with Israel, but that neither would he tolerate active attempts to undermine it. The liberal retrenchment by the palace was most acutely felt in terms of a range of new constraints on press freedom. Examples were made of the more outspoken Arabic weekly papers in order to encourage the reintroduction of self-censorship among journalists and editors. The success of the policy can be seen by Jordan's lowly ranking of 128 out of 173 countries in the Reporters Without Borders' 2008 Worldwide Press Freedom Index. New pressure points were applied to the professional associations in Jordan, crucibles of political activism in the past. The general intelligence, the main part of the national security state but one which was not subject to any meaningful process of accountability in the wake of the kingdom's financial problems, remained an unfettered institutional support of the monarchy. The climate of reform associated with the extended 'Amman spring' of 1989–93 had been replaced by a new era of constrained liberalism from above.

Since the early 1990s other leaders have discovered ways in which such controlled reform could be made to work to their benefit. Through much of the decade Yemen acquired a reputa-tion for open elections and press freedoms, even though President Ali Abdullah Saleh's grip on central power has not diminished, and the voluntary union between North Yemen and South Yemen in 1990 was only consolidated through civil war in 1994. Yasser Arafat returned to Palestine in 1994, as part of the peace process with Israel to enhance his standing through election to be the president of the newly created Palestinian Authority. His supporters subsequently dominated the Palestinian Legislative Council, also through the mechanism of elections.

With a brief delay, this strategy was even adopted in the Gulf states. Prior to the early 1990s Kuwait was the only emirate that satisfied even Washington's nominal conditions of democratisa-tion, being the only Gulf state with an elected assembly. And that was an exercise in institution building that was seriously flawed: an appointed component to the assembly; no legalised political parties as such; a small and restricted male-only franchise of around 110,000 (out of a total population of two million), and with the assembly dissolved by the emir for long periods in the recent past (1976–80 and 1986–92). Following independence in 1971, Bahrain was briefly governed according to a liberal constitution, which resulted in just one parliamentary election in 1973 before being shelved two years later. By the turn of the new millennium the Gulf had witnessed institutional proliferation: an elected municipal council and an elected national council in Qatar; an elected legislative council and an appointed upper chamber in Bahrain; an appointed consultative council in Abu Dhabi; an assembly based on a combination of appointment and election in Oman; and those limited elections for the Riyadh municipal council in Saudi Arabia. In short, there had been a festival of the ceremonials of modern represen-tational politics, with an appreciative West looking on, but with little discernible improvement in the substantive nature of governance.

Explaining the absence of democratisation

Since the fall of Communism in Europe and its impact on the developing world, a debate has emerged about why the Middle East has apparently remained largely impervious to such forces of change. Possible explanations put forward have included: the colonial legacy; Islam as a belief system; the state-dependent nature of potentially democratising classes. This debate has not reached a clear conclusion. Rather, it has divided commentators on the region. The assumptions on which the debate has been founded have betrayed the biases of those taking part. Moreover, the conclusions emanating from the debate have often been exploited to reaffirm political allegiances, with strong policy implications, especially felt along the Arab/Palestinian–Israeli fault-line.

Take the notion of civil society, for example. It was the growth of civil society in Eastern Europe as a result of the 'Helsinki process' in the 1970s that led to the emergence of such robust organisations as the Solidarity trade union in Poland, Charter 77 in Czechoslovakia and New Forum in East Germany. It was the growing popularity of such bodies and their independent nature from the Communist state that helped to weaken the ruling regimes and, with the withdrawal of Soviet military power, eventually precipitated their downfall. The existence of a healthy and vibrant civil society has consequently been cited as a precondition for democratic reform elsewhere in the world. But a question hangs in the air: does the Middle East have a thriving civil society or not?

Posing such a question immediately requires a definition of the term, in order that we may know for what we are looking. But there is no such agreed definition. Rather, minimal and maximal conceptions vie for attention. The former would look something like this: 'civil society is the associational space that exists between the state and the individual'. The beauty of such a definition is that it is brief, clear and inclusive of all group activities separate from and hence not beholden to the state. In a region where many political problems may be traced to the size, dominance and aggressiveness of the state, anything that helps widen the gap between the individual and the state, and acts as a political shock absorber has the potential to play a valuable role in reform. Crucially, such an approach would allow tribes and religious organisations to be considered part of civil society.

A cursory look at regional experience would suggest that according to this definition-lite there is a range of experience in the region. Not only are different Middle Eastern states distributed at various points along that continuum, but they have shifted position both moderately and dramatically over time, dependent on various historical and regime experiences. So, for example, Iraq under Saddam Hussein would have left comparatively little space for independent associationalism; a repressive, authoritarian state squeezing the space for civil societal activism. Palestinian experience, on the other hand, with its various political factions and the highly politicised nature of the Occupied Territories, would, by contrast, be viewed as having a comparatively large space for pluralist associationalism. This at least was true prior to the petrified bipolarity that the post-2006 Fatah–Hamas struggle has imposed upon it.

The maximal conception of civil society would look very different, however. The point of departure would be one that contains a strong individualistic gloss, because of the inherent liberalism that underpins the political process in the West. Such a definition would look something like this: 'civil society consists of non-state associationalism, where those groups conform to standards of civility and tolerance, exist independent of the wishes of the state and where membership is rendered voluntarily'. In terms of the Middle East, such a definition would require not merely that associations exist to buttress the individual, but that they conform to acceptable standards of political correctness. In contrast to the minimal definition, the inclusion of tribes and religious organisations would be regarded as problematic, the former because it could be claimed that they are not based on voluntary but primordial membership, the latter because many would be viewed as insufficiently inclusive of a feminist or gay agenda.

The stakes involved in this definitionally driven debate are considerable. Loading up the definition of civil society in this way would be more likely to lead to the conclusion that civil society in the region is absent or only present in an extremely fragile form. By extension that would mean that the potential for political reform, let alone democratisation, was low. This is basically the position of the pro-Israel lobby in the US, American support for the Jewish state being in large part based on a convergence of values between the two countries and their societies, of which democracy is a leading and robust component. Continuing evidence that the rest of the region does not share the values of the US has constrained a more even-handed approach, especially towards the Arab world.

Civil society is only one way of explaining the absence of democratisation in the Middle East. The colonial inheritance is a second. This explanation is beloved of many in the region as well as of left of centre commentators. It sees the nature of the contemporary Middle Eastern state and the state system as a whole as the product of European colonialism. It points to the particular priorities of state building as the bulwark of this system. European powers invested heavily in the creation of a centralised, rather than a decentralised, state, with ministries, government agencies and a capital city as the expression of newly established power configurations. In short, they created centralised, coercive rather than liberal states, with investment flowing disproportionately into the creation of new police forces and different branches of the conventional military.

The main problem with the colonial inheritance as an explanation of the absence of open government is its historically specific nature. It is nearly forty years since the UAE became fully independent, the last major territories in the region to do so. It is between fifty and sixty years since national revolutions took place in countries like Egypt and Syria. In the intervening time elites and societies have had the opportunity to transform the polities in which they reside. And indeed much transformation has taken place. If this transformation has not included liberalisation and democratisation then one must conclude that at very least there is an insufficient consensus on the direction of reform, accompanied by a further insufficiency of collective will. Indeed, ruling regimes have deployed the considerable state power at their disposal to ensure that their authority is not eroded through substantive reform. In the meantime, the colonial inheritance remains the ultimate alibi for inaction.

'LIBYA'S MASSOCRACY'

There are few regimes in the Arab world where the gap between the rhetoric and practice of good governance is more stark than in Libya's State of the Masses (*jamahiriya*). Once he had consolidated power, Libyan leader Colonel Muamar Qadhafi preached the virtues of participatory democracy in his own quixotic theory of government, the Third Universal Theory. He dissolved the country's ministries as being too distant from ordinary people, replacing them with General People's Committees. He introduced a system of direct participation through a hierarchy of people's congresses, which channelled views and ideas upwards to the General People's Congress at the apex of the political order. In reality, views were sometimes freely expressed, especially at a local level and as far as primarily economic issues were concerned. On political matters the system was much less benign. A parallel structure of zealous but unaccountable Revolutionary Committees monitored the congresses and inhibited debate on matters of state. Opposition

'LIBYA'S MASSOCRACY' (*cont.*)

figures have been executed, forced into exile and then hunted down. Meanwhile, in spite of having no formal position other than 'Guide of the First of September Revolution', Qadhafi bestrides the system. Political parties are banned as being divisive. Qadhafi favours his own tribe, which hales from the centre of the country, enabling him to maintain a political balancing act between the traditional regional rivals in the west and east of the country. He indulges his offspring, as so many rulers in the region do, who divide into two categories, wasters and regime apparatchiks. One son, the appropriately named Hannibal, sparked a diplomatic incident between Libya and Switzerland after a fracas in a Geneva hotel in 2008. Libya retaliated against the hapless Swiss by withdrawing large deposits from its banks, cutting oil deliveries and closing its company offices in Tripoli.

For those who believe that the barriers to democratisation and good governance are particularly ingrained, a belief system explanation is attractive because it appears to offer a cultural rationale for the region's resistance to change. Islam is not the only belief system explanation that can be introduced into the discussion, the existence of a tribal or patriarchal society offer alternatives. Islam, however, remains the most controversial and oft debated belief system barrier. After-all, Islam is the religion of the vast majority of the region's population; it still commands widespread personal adherence as a religion. The word Islam itself means 'submission', implying a quietism that can be projected from the personal to the macro-political. Interestingly, Islamist conceptions of faith politics confirm such a perspective. Islamists agree with the proposition that Islam is a barrier to democratisation. They maintain that it is to God that one should look for a blueprint of politics not man. More specifically, they regard the sovereignty of God rather than the sovereignty of the people as the source of political authority.

Those critical of the Islamic belief-system approach in explaining the absence of democratisation usually base their refutation on the claim that it 'essentialises' Islam. In other words, it sees the approach as boiling down religion to a single and monolithic form, with little chance of variable outcomes. The criticism is overdone. Western liberal academics and commentators living in a secular world in a post-Christian age are hardly well placed to judge the profundity of the impact of Islam as a belief system. However, it is helpful to be warned of the perils of religious determinism. There have after-all been important experiences of democratising movements in the region, such as the 1906 Constitutional revolution in Iran, even if these developments were not ultimately strong enough to drive through successful transitions in the nature of governance.

Other claims marshalled against the Islam belief system barrier are more mixed. The idea that Islam contains elements within it that are resonant of democratisation are contentious at best. Many would see the importance of consultation (*shura*), a strong invocation within Islam, as a wise course for rulers to take, but a pale and ultimately distracting alternative to widespread mobilisation and participation. In any case, for every apparently benign aspect of democratisation in Islam there is one that is more autocratic. The oft quoted Islamic thinker Ibn Taymiya maintained that it is better to endure 100 years of despotism than one year of chaos (*fitna*).

Similarly, the claim that hundreds of millions of Muslims are already vigorous participants in the democracies of the world is again contentious at best. Muslims may participate within democratic systems in Western countries, but that is where an explicit democratic political culture is already deeply embedded. Judgements about the extent of the power of democratic social-isation are variable. Democratic systems in Bangladesh and Pakistan have proven to be fragile, and periodically compro-mised by the intrusion of unaccountable actors, such as the military; Malaysia, though not unproblematic, less so. The more successful examples of democratic transition among majority Muslim states are still in their infancy, notably in Indonesia. In the Middle East itself, Morocco has taken some important steps in a liberal direction since 2000, but the palace still retains a powerful veto over substantive change. Turkey is undoubtedly the region's best performer, though even there at its best democracy has required qualification, as it does today.

A danger with the belief system explanation is the difficulty of identifying when such a reality might change and to be able to explain why. Latin Americanists point out that a traditionalist form of Roman Catholicism was still being invoked to explain the absence of democracy in the Iberian Peninsula and Latin America in the late 1960s, even as those societies began to enter a period of robust democratic transformation. In a globalising world, where good governance is increasingly identified as inclusive of democratisation, there are multiple reminders of what political structures and processes are expected across the world, the Middle East included. Though such globalising values have far to go in rivalling well entrenched belief systems, there can be little doubt as to how such values should be packaged if they are to impact the region, namely in a way that is culturally appropriate and sensitised.

Democratisation theory holds that the process of transformation is more likely to take place when there is a coherent and well-organised stratum in society that identifies its interests as embodied in such change. In Western Europe, democratic transition is often identified with the rise of the middle classes, especially that of a commercial bourgeoisie. In much of the Middle East, such class patterns have not been replicated. Ironically, a middle class does exist. Indeed, with a relatively small industrial working class and no landed upper class any longer to speak of, the middle class is a relatively large and often affluent one. The problems, however, are related to its component parts, their divided interests and the limited nature of their organisation.

If a private sector and state-independent middle class best reflects the fortunes of the class in a European context, the experiences of the Middle East are very different. Far and away the largest component of the middle class in the region is the bureaucratic bourgeoisie, that part of the class that is wholly dependent on the state for its employment and material affluence. It has benefited from the inexorable expansion of the state, both resulting from the ideological changes of the 1950s and the era of huge oil revenues in the 1970s. The problem with such a stratum from the perspective of democratic change is that it tends to be loyal to the state that remunerates it. The conservative nature of the bureaucratic bourgeoisie is evident in the Egyptian case, where it has scuppered successive attempts at economic reform since the 1980s by fighting an anti-reformist policy rearguard.

Other fractions of the middle class do exist in the region. There is an industrial middle class, of sorts, though this is small in size; there remains a deep-seated reluctance to invest long term in fixed assets for fear of the uncertainty of returns. The commercial bourgeoisie is more numerous than its industrial equivalent, but it too is likely to be dependent on the state, especially if it requires access to state controlled foreign currency or state dispensed import licenses in order to be able to trade. Parts of the professional middle class are state dependent, for example doctors working in state hospitals and teachers working in state run schools. But then parts of it are not, as many operate exclusively in the private sector, there being both a private health and education sector. The fragmented nature of the professional middle class is underlined by the fact that there is a third category of professional who does both.

There are many doctors, engineers and lawyers active in the politics of the region, but this tends to manifest itself in ideological and party politics, rather than as a class perspective towards the state. In the Middle East, the state remains a bulwark against reform, unshakably so as long as resources remain so overwhelmingly at its disposal.

The Middle East has struggled with the art of governance. Regional opinion proved to be finely honed in terms of what sort of system it did not want to be ruled by, resisting the last vestiges of colonialism and struggling for national revolution. But reaching consensus on what to replace it with has been altogether more vexing. Rule by soldiers, once the hope of the masses, was discredited by incompetence and self-indulgence. After the 1960s political regimes have proved to be more cynical in their motives for government, but also more difficult to dislodge. Regimes have entrenched themselves in power, deploying a combination of oil wealth to incentivise loyal behaviour, and repression to enforce it. As regimes became increasingly 'fierce' with their own populations so a passive disengagement from politics proved increasingly to be the norm among the peoples of such states.

Some political reform was achieved in the region between the late 1980s and mid-1990s, as countries across the region found themselves to be victims of a fiscal crunch. In some cases, this was exacerbated by street violence. A period of political reformism as a palliative for falling living standards ensued. Many of the more potent aspects of reform have been quietly clawed back as the original conditions that triggered them have receded. The region was sluggish and wary when the opportunity of the great global opening presented itself in the mid to late 1980s. There has been an instinctive suspicion of externally backed schemes for reform, especially those emanating from the US. Yet regimes have appreciated that in a globalising world change in the direction of the good governance agenda is required. This has primarily been dispensed from above. Public opinion has largely looked on at the cautious reforms from above which have typified the 1990s, bystanders in their own lands.

7
Leadership

In the second half of the twentieth century the dominant image of leadership in the Middle East was of the brutal autocrat, exercising power arbitrarily at the expense of a downtrodden population. Such a view was a product of two things: first, a tendency to conflate historical experience and to assume that the medieval exercise of power familiar from such stories as the Crusades and the fictional *One Thousand and One Nights* was an accurate backdrop to the contemporary era; second, a tendency to generalise the nature of contemporary leadership from the appearance of 'big man' politics in the post-colonial world in general and the Middle East in particular. Because of their domination of the headlines it was easy to assume that the likes of Nasser of Egypt, the PLO leader Yasser Arafat and the dictators of Baghdad and Damascus, Saddam Hussein and Hafez al-Asad respectively, best represented the nature of leadership, certainly in the Arab world. However, as we shall see, this approach involved the confusion of more than one leadership style. Even the Asad and Saddam cases were not as straightforward as they appeared to be.

Asad and Saddam

There is no doubt that there were aspects of the rule of Saddam Hussein and Hafez al-Asad that were recognisably tyrannical by the standards of almost any era. Both were guilty of developing and sitting atop a police state; both squeezed the space for independent political action; both presided over the emergence of a plethora of corrupt practices, devoid of the scrutiny of any independent body, that is to say devoid of the rule of law.

It could be argued that the despotic essence of both their regimes was a function of the social origins of both men and the nature of the political challenges they faced. Both Saddam Hussein and Hafez al-Asad were from rural, peasant areas – Tikrit and Qardaha respectively – where livelihoods were marginal and life coarse. Both came from minorities, routinely and casually discriminated against by earlier manifestations of state power, and scraping an existence at the social margins, Saddam as one of the twenty per cent Sunni Arabs in a majority Shia society, Asad as a member of the eleven per cent Alawi community in a majority Sunni Arab environment. Both rose rapidly from their obscure and unpromising backgrounds through involvement in revolutionary politics at a time of profound national and regional political ferment and the consequent rapid turnover in governing elites, Saddam through the civilian section of the Ba'th Party, Asad through its military faction. Having travelled so far to reach the top of the political hierarchy neither man was willing to relinquish their new-found status without a struggle. For Saddam in particular, who had been imprisoned in the early 1960s, the lesson learnt was that misplaced mercy simply gives one's rivals another chance to win power.

Saddam owed his rapid promotion after the Ba'thist coup of July 1968 to his ability to organise the internal security of the regime, or, to be more precise, that part of the regime loyal to his patron, Ahmad Hasan al-Bakr, the original coup leader. By 1971 President Bakr had promoted his young protégé to be the deputy secretary-general of the party with responsibility for internal security. Only once it was too late would President Bakr recognise the dangers of having a deputy who had eliminated all effective counterweights within the party and the revolutionary institutions of power. In 1979 Bakr 'resigned' on the grounds of ill health, and was succeeded at once by his former deputy, Saddam. The change in part reflected the need to shore up power in response to the Iranian revolution that had delivered regime change in Tehran in January 1979. There was no room for faint hearts in Baghdad, as Saddam's regime began to try to contain the Iranian revolution for the sake of its own existence, but also on behalf of the wider Arab Sunni region, and indeed the wider world.

Asad's fitness to rule was in many ways a product of the stability that he brought, in this case to Syria as a whole rather than simply the organisation of regime power. Following two decades of chronic domestic discontinuity, and the policy incoherence that accompanied it, Asad's so-called Correctionist Movement brought to an end the political spasms that seemed to convulse the Syrian body politic more or less every other year. Because of the narrow confessional base of his social origins, Asad worked to expand the coalition of support under-pinning his regime. Other minorities such as the Christians were brought in, as were the peasantry of Latakia and beyond. Even Sunni Arabs from modest backgrounds such as (vice-president) Abdul Halim Khaddam, Mustafa Tlas (defence minister) and Hikmet Shihabi (chief of staff), were added to an increasingly broadly based coalition of power. This helped to ameliorate the minoritarian appearance of the regime in general, and that which still prevails at the security core of the regime in the form of fifty to sixty senior Alawi enforcers, known colloquially in Syria as the 'barons'.

In spite of his attempt to broaden the base of his authority, the Ba'thist regime found itself locked into an increasingly unforgiving struggle with the Muslim Brotherhood, which had come to represent the lower middle class Arab Sunnis, largely left out of Asad's new coalition. With the political milieu one of centralised authoritarianism, increasingly the brotherhood came to oppose the regime on its own grounds, utilising similar methods of repression. Violence began to define the regime-opposition dynamic from 1978, with sporadic attacks on the symbols and personnel of the regime. The struggle came to a head in the central city of Hama in 1982, where the brotherhood determined to make a stand, presumably in the hope of triggering sympathetic uprisings elsewhere in the country. Such a calculation proved to be badly misconceived, and they were no match for the heavy weapons of the regime, encamped around the city. Between 5000 and 20,000 Syrian Islamists and their supporters perished in the confrontation, which as a by-product destroyed the old city of Hama. Though it arguably had little choice if it wished to survive, the Syrian regime was nonetheless guilty of one of the great massacres of the modern era.

The Saddamist regime is less associated with one major act of violence like Hama. Saddam's twenty-four years in power were continuously punctuated by a range and variety of the uses of violence. These included: the killing of large numbers of clan members of elite families who were in an implacable opposition to the regime, such as the Hakim family of Shia clerics; the grisly torture of party and military men who had unwisely dabbled (or were accused of so doing) in political conspiracies; swift and savage retribution against village and neighbourhood communities from whom assassination attempts on the leader had emanated. Saddam even delighted in showing off such acts of retribution, notably his circulation of a video of the 1979 special convention of the Ba'th Party Regional Command meeting, during which a number of real or perceived rivals were led away, the best known of some 500 apparatchiks, purged for being deemed insufficiently loyal to the new order. If Saddam does have 'a Hama', however, it is the use of chemical weapons against the Iraqi Kurds at Halabja in March 1988, during the latter stages of the Iran–Iraq war. With some 4000 women, children and old men having perished in a collective retribution for the Kurds' alliance with Iran, Halabja soon went down in human rights lore as the application of industrial strength munitions by the Iraqi regime against its fellow citizens.

The problem with generalising about leadership in the Arab world from individuals like Saddam Hussein and Hafez al-Asad is that it tends to emphasise one aspect of leadership, the use of repressive violence. As we have seen, even the Asad regime in Syria did not use violence as a critical determinant of regime survival on a more or less continuous basis in the way that it might be claimed that the Saddamist regime did. Asad used other, more subtle and ultimately more effective devices, such as the construction of a broadly based coalition of power. In other words, though violence did feature in the Syria of the 1970s and 1980s it did not exclusively define the actions and policies of the regime. Even in Saddam's Iraq violence, though generally ever present, was not the only tactic of choice for the leader. When in the early 1990s Saddam Hussein struggled to maintain the base of his regime after his defeat in Kuwait and decided to incorporate the Sunni Arab tribes into his corner he chose humility over intimidation. Saddam travelled to the tribal areas of the west and north-west of the country in order to apologise in their presence for the early anti-tribal policies of the Ba'thist regime. To see the Saddam regime as purely engaged in a medieval orgy of violence would be to make such a development literally inconceivable.

To suggest that violence was somehow the defining characteristic of leadership is to risk losing sensitivity to other key aspects. It is also dangerously dehumanising to regard a people as best defined by the use of violence. Political leadership can be broken down into at least five key component parts: the acquisition of political power; the management of elite relations; the relationship with the masses; the development and implementation of policy especially in the arena of high politics (notably foreign and defence policy); political succession. It is in relation to these components of leadership that we will focus on a range of four typical leadership styles prevalent in the region: the founder-leader; the big man; the negotiated leadership; and the institutional leader.

The founder-leader

With the modern state system only created in the 1920s, the period of decolonisation dating from the 1940s/1950s and the post-colonial shakedown in political power having taken place in the 1950s/1960s it is hardly surprising that the founder-leader phenomenon is a strong one and easily recalled in the Middle East. In this way, the region reflects the developing world more generally. In Black Africa the founder-leader concept is also a solid one through men like Kwame Nkrumah (Ghana), Jomo Kenyatta (Kenya) and Julius Nyerere (Tanzania). Elsewhere in the world other names quickly come to mind, some illustrious, some less: Nehru (India); Mao (China); and Castro (Cuba). In the Middle East the existence of a founder of an important regime is more important than whether the founder-leader chooses to refer to himself as a 'king' or 'president'. We should therefore be wary of categorising leadership along such formalistic lines. Abdul Aziz ibn Saud, who re-established the Saudi state in the early twentieth century, was as much of a founder-leader as was Colonel Nasser of Egypt, who founded the country's first genuinely independent regime. This similarity exists regardless of the fact that their titles were that of 'king' and 'president' respectively.

The advent of the founder-leader is usually associated with a momentous event or founding myth, the moment at which a leader or dynasty came to power, or when the greatness of a founding figure was realised. For Al Saud it was the recapture of Riyadh in 1902, the seat of political power in central Arabia, but one from which Al Saud had been excluded since the fall of the previous Saudi political entity in Arabia in 1891. By seizing Riyadh from his main rivals, the Rashid clan, Abdul Aziz opened the way for the conquest of the interior of the Arabian peninsula. This would eventually encompass the Islamic holy sites in the north-west, and what would later be discovered to be the large oil reservoirs of the Eastern Province. For Nasser's Egypt, the founding event was the Free Officers Movement and the seizing of power in what would come to be the national revolution of 1952. This was the rock upon which Nasser's subsequent victories would be based: the successful assertion of an independent Arab foreign and security policy, and the political defeat of Britain and France at Suez in 1956.

In most cases elite management was more complex and reciprocal than one might have expected of these dominant leadership figures. In Saudi Arabia before the onset of stratospheric oil income, tribal culture was effectively the political culture of the kingdom. This meant that an individual's fitness to rule had to be proven and reaffirmed, and could not be taken for granted once achieved. The hierarchy of power was a flat one. Abdul Aziz incorporated the tribal peripheries of his new state by binding them to the centre through his marriage to the daughters of leading tribal figures. By this simple, traditional device he gave all of the major tribes an interest in the perpetuation of the newly established order. This explains why many of the senior princes in the country today are half-brothers. Nasser's creation of political institutions like the Liberation Rally, the National Union and the Arab Socialist Union showed his appreciation of the need to institutionalise regime power. But it also points to his deep unwillingness to cede real control, even to those closest to him. The creation and subsequent dismantling of the first two institutions just listed reflect this underlying suspicion. Nasser's fears of an army coup, even at the hands of one of his oldest political and personal friends, Field Marshall Abdul Hakim Amr, the head of the army, indicated his nervousness even at one so close. In the end, Amr was allowed (or required) to take political responsibility for the defeat in the 1967 war, which involved his suicide, whether real or apparent.

The relationship between the founder-leaders and the people is difficult to measure in retrospect, but tends to have been a positive one, because of the contributions that they have made to state building. Nasser was arguably the only Arab leader to enjoy an uncontested popular legitimacy throughout most if not all of his political career. Remarkably, this legitimacy was not confined to Egypt itself. It was even felt for long periods of time in the 1950s and 1960s across the wider region. This was achieved in part through the stirring demagoguery of his long, unscripted, set-piece speeches, which were carried by the Voice of the Arabs (*Sawt al-Arab*) radio station, the internet of its day. In part, it was a reflection of Nasser's political successes. At last it looked as though a regional figure existed who could deliver on the expectations of the people. If Nasser was very much a man of the people, who caught and expressed their often intangible political aspirations, Abdul Aziz was a man motivated initially by narrower, clan concerns. As his ambitions grew, so he had to forge an inclusive approach to governance or face the destabilising impact of revolts at the periphery. Though many in the expanding state would not have instinctively identified with Abdul Aziz, his successful wielding of military and the beginnings of administrative power quickly began to command respect. His reputation as a state-builder was soon assured.

Founder-leaders have dealt with the challenge of policy-making in different institutional ways, but few have ignored it. The Al Saud dynasty has tended to take the major portfolios of state for itself. In recent times, the position of prime minister is held by the king. The post of his senior deputy accrues to his heir apparent. Other top cabinet positions are earmarked for senior royals, notably defence, interior and foreign affairs. The princes assigned to such portfolios have treated them as fiefdoms, with many of them held by the same princes for up to four decades. This shows how closely associated state, regime and government is in the kingdom. While this has given the senior princes a close and continuing input into policy, the absence of commoners in many of the highest positions, who are easier to sack if policy goes awry, has robbed them of a policy lightning rod. Nasser was clearly the dominant decision-maker in Egypt as far as foreign policy was concerned. He was advised by a very small group of confidents, which included the famous mouth-piece of the regime, the journalist Muhammad Hassanein Heikal, a venerable figure still providing political commentary in the twenty-first century. Nasser seemed more at home with the broad conceptual issues of the day, like imperialism and revolu-tion, where problems were more black and white, and less cluttered by detail as was the arena of domestic policy. The latter was more the subject of cabinet government, the successive administrations containing a large number of former military officers, reflecting the preoccupations of the day.

Only in the area of political succession does the monarchi-cal-republican regime division appear to offer markedly differing outcomes. In the case of the former, founder-leaders expect a dynastic succession and their authority usually carries the day. There was no doubt that Abdul Aziz ibn Saud would be followed as king by one of his direct descendants. It was the logic of a newly invigorated clan-oriented politics, and one that could not practically have been contested from within the system. The fact that Abdul Aziz's successor, King Saud, proved to be a weak and ineffectual leader at a time when external challenges were multiplying, shows how an ordered succession does not always result in an optimal outcome. In the case of Abdul Aziz, his immediate successor was removed in 1964 in favour of the next senior son, Faisal, a man who had already demonstrated his abilities in government and whose religious authority gave him an appeal not shared by his siblings. Succession problems have proved to be more numerous in the radical republics. This was even the case in Nasser's Egypt, where neither leader nor system had been open to serious opposition. In Nasser's case, it was the dangers of a quick and unexpected succession, where contingency arrangements were largely absent, that was the problem, a heart attack removing the Egyptian leader unexpectedly at the age of fifty-two. By recourse to the constitution, the regime was able to stabilise the system at a point of acute uncertainty. This allowed Anwar Sadat, a free officer and next in the protocol line in his capacity as vice-president, to take charge of the transitional stage of leadership. It also allowed him by stealth and much against expectation to deepen and then consolidate his own hold on power, a hold that would last for twelve years.

THE ASAD SUCCESSION

President Asad had long envisaged a dynastic succession, but it was his eldest son, Basil, who was being groomed to take over. With his dashing style and equestrian success, Basil certainly looked the part. Sudden death in a car crash removed Basil from the scene in 1994, whereupon the president looked for an alternative. He fixed on his third child, Bashar, a quiet and bookish man who was training in London to be an ophthalmologist. Like Rajiv Gandhi summoned home by Indira Gandhi after the death of her favourite son, Sanjay, a couple of decades before, Bashar had no choice in the matter when he received his father's call. Poster photographs of Hafez, Bashar and Basil – 'the father, son and holy ghost' – began to appear in confirmation of the new arrangement. An apprenticeship in the army and responsibility for the Lebanon political 'file' then followed. Furthermore, Bashar cultivated the younger royals across the Arab region. His father began the task of removing the old guard – the men that Bashar would have spent his life referring to as 'uncle' – in order to bolster his young son's

THE ASAD SUCCESSION (*cont.*)

authority. He was only half able to complete the job. When the succession came, however, it passed from Hafez to Bashar without trouble. The constitution had to be amended in order to change the clause insisting that the head of state be forty years of age. (Bashar was thirty-four.) The young Asad needed to be confirmed in office by the party and the parliament, but that proved to be a formality. The regime had renewed itself and its ambitious senior members had found it expedient to unite behind another man called Asad. Eight years later, 'Dr Bashar' as he is widely known in an expression of modernistic respect, remains in office, without the broad authority of his father, but with more to him than many had thought possible upon his accession.

The 'big man' leader

The big man leader is resonant of the dominant individual leader model, but where the big man has little or none of the legitimising raw material of the founder-leader. This legitimacy deficit is perhaps best seen in the area of charisma, one of renowned sociologist Max Weber's great legitimisers of leadership. While founder-leaders like Nasser are likely to have charismatic personalities, the big man is much less so. It is possible to try to manufacture charisma using the institutions of the state. Monopolising state broadcasting is within the grasp of any leader, no matter how dull, if they hold political power. Saturation coverage of the big man, on broadcast media, prominently in the front pages of the press and in poster form, is assumed to compensate for real inspiration.

Again, this is a familiar story of the developing world, especially following the passing of the first generation of founder-leaders. Comparable examples would include: Daniel arap Moi (Kenya) and Mobuto Sese Seko (Zaire). There is no shortage of such leaders from the recent history of the Middle East. A representative sample would include: Abdul Karim al-Qassim (Iraq, 1958–63); King Saud bin Abdul Aziz (Saudi Arabia, 1953–64); Shah Mohammed Reza Shah (Iran, 1941–79); Anwar Sadat (Egypt, 1970–81). Middle East incumbent leaders most appropriate to this description would include: Husni Mubarak (Egypt, 1981–); Ali Abdullah Saleh (Yemen, 1978–); Omar al-Bashir (Sudan, 1989–); Zine El Abidine Ben Ali (Tunisia, 1987–).

Few of these 'big figures' came to power as a result of a momentous event in which they played a starring role, unlike the founder-leaders. For example, the Pahlavi dynasty had been established before Mohammed Reza Shah's time, dating from his father's takeover of power in 1924. Worse still, in 1953 the Shah was temporarily driven out of the country by a nationalist wave, led by the supporters of the iconic figure, Mohammed Mossadeq. The Shah only owed his restoration as monarch soon after to the strength of foreign powers, notably the Americans, rather than to his own skills or popularity. The fundamental illegitimacy of the Shah's hold on power may be dated from that day. It preoccupied him throughout the twenty-six years of the rest of his reign, and helps explain many of his subsequently more nationalist gestures, such as the seizure of three strategic Arab islands in the Gulf waterway in 1971. In Egypt, Husni Mubarak came to power because of the unexpected assassination of his predecessor, Anwar Sadat. The fact that Mubarak held the position of vice-president meant that he enjoyed a formal position of primacy, which he was able to turn to his own advantage. His background as the former head of the Egyptian air force made him acceptable to the country's powerful military. In the wake of what could have been political turmoil, Mubarak as president was a safe and steady choice.

The management of elites is usually more difficult for this category of leader because of the largely arbitrary way in which they have come to power. The 'if him, why not me?' rule prevails in spades in a republic, but also within the relevant circles inside a monarchy. The Shah was contemptuous of the political elites in Iran, dismissing those with any credibility, and choosing to surround himself with technocrats and yes-men. This meant that while he enjoyed an illusion of power, in fact he was oblivious to many of the undercurrents in his own country. By the time he attempted to retrieve the situation, by appointing as prime minister the respected nationalist, Shapour Bakhtiar, a matter of days before his ouster, his position was already an impossible one. In Mubarak's Egypt, the space for legal political activism and discourse has been dominated by the government party, the National Democratic Party (NDP). Rather than being an effective and cohesive movement to support the president it has become moribund and self-serving over the years, only latterly in part revived as a base of support for the president's son. The NDP has dominated the country's sluggish parliament, winning successive national elections and ensuring Mubarak's continued nomination as president. With the only political alternatives the illegal but partially tolerated Muslim Brotherhood, a cluster of small and vulnerable centre parties, and political disengagement, Mubarak has for many been the only political game in town.

Authoritarianism was a well-established political strategy for the big man leader in the Middle East, especially in the 1970s and 1980s. The Shah used his secret police, SAVAK, to intimidate and deter. Even among Iranian students abroad, the West included, SAVAK enjoyed a fearsome reputation. The Shah's regime made use of a wide range of devices to weaken his opponents, from exile to extra-judicial killing. Husni Mubarak has at times been a small steps reformer (and at others a small steps anti-reformer), with the slight opening and closing of political opportunities a reflection of cautious regime threat perceptions. The structural incrementalism of the Mubarak period has often seemed like a deliberate attempt to distance himself from the zeal for change of his two predecessors. This has generally kept his period of rule free from the policy lurches of Nasser and Sadat. It was as if Egypt, at first at least, had had enough of the charisma at the top identified with his republican predecessors, and needed some of the ballast that only dourness can bring.

The problem with authoritarianism and centralisation at the level of high politics is that it cannot then be relaxed when it comes down to policy-making. This, together with the centrally planned, state-led model that prevailed between the 1950s and the 1980s, meant that there were frequently policy bottlenecks, delaying the formulation and implementation of policy, and unintegrated and contradictory policy outputs. In the Shah's Iran the system was so centralised, and the stratum of political functionaries so narrow, that it hardly functioned at all without his active input. He became the architect of domestic reform and regional strategy alike. The onset of the Shah's cancer in the final months of the regime hobbled the regime's ability to fight back against the revolutionary challenge. Under Mubarak, policy-making has often been painfully slow and prone to reversals, especially as the bureaucracy has sought to block various attempts to introduce economic reform, viewing this as inimical to its own interests. The responsibility for stunting reform has even been assumed by the presidency itself, as Mubarak has always placed political stability ahead of the assumed advantages of economic liberalisation. The experience of bread riots under his predecessor in 1977 taught Mubarak and his generation a clear lesson: not to trifle with the stability of the country, even if trying to please such bodies as the IMF.

The fate of many of these big men is to have power ripped from them before they are able fully to consider the issue of succession. Relative longevity in power is not necessarily evidence of a secure base, as the Shah of Iran found to his cost, after more than three decades. Clan links have rarely been unimportant in the region with respect to political power. As the Shah left Iran for the last time he vainly tried to seek a future role for his infant son. Husni Mubarak has been manoeuvring for a dynastic republican succession, in spite of denials that this is his objective. His actions, however, betray that his favoured successor is his second son, Gamal, who, after working in London as a banker, returned home to became a public figure in 2000. Since then Gamal has set about trying to modernise the NDP. He has also attempted to reform the Egyptian economy from a newly created policy office in the upper echelons of his father's party. President Mubarak's decision in 2004 to eschew the older generation and appoint a cabinet of younger reformers more in keeping with his son's ideas showed how prepared the incumbent was to contribute to his son's advancement. The dynastic succession in Syria, itself also a radical republic of old, has clearly encouraged him in his goal.

The negotiated leadership

While the founder-leader and big man types might be the more instantly recognisable forms of leadership in the modern Middle East it would be misleading to suggest that that is the whole story. There is more to the region than the 'leader as political system' experience. The first two types tend to attract the greater attention, not least because of their notoriety, for example through their association with human rights abuses and concerns over standards of good governance. Nevertheless, more cooperative, collegiate and institutionalised approaches to leadership do also exist in the Middle East and should not be ignored.

An important aspect of this falls into the category of negotiated leadership. The main point of this variant is that leadership is not seized through a violent power play or military takeover but is acquired as a result of an intra-regime bargain. This is likely to be the product of a negotiation between the representatives of important internal regime constituents. The outcome can then be legitimised using whatever instruments have most traction within the societies concerned, traditional, ideological or even constitutional ones. Examples of comparable experiences around the developing world would include: the establishment of a collective leadership in Yugoslavia after Tito's death in 1980; the succession from Nelson Mandela to Thabo Mbeki in South Africa in 1999; and President Nyerere standing down in Tanzania in 1985. Regional illustrations would include: the choice of Khalid (1975–82) and Fahd (1982–2005) as kings in Saudi Arabia; the agreement on governance sharing after 1938 between the al-Ahmad and the al-Salim branches of the Sabah family in Kuwait.

In all of these cases the negotiated nature of leadership reflected a widely shared unease at recently experienced intra-elite dynamics. These tended to be characterised by such features as intense competition, simmering antipathy and even limited conflict. The Saudi senior princes chose Prince Khalid as an act of healing. They did so in spite of his limited senior administrative experience, or even interest in the routine responsibilities of being ruler, normally essential characteristics of a meritocratic choice. His attractions to the clan as the new monarch were precisely because of his calming effect on intra-family dynamics, not wider issues of policy or strategy. These were: first, that he was able to ameliorate the trauma felt by the assassination of his predecessor, King Faisal, by one of his nephews; second, that Khalid was seen as a force for unity after the raw and damaging struggle which had racked the clan and its principals, Saud and Faisal, a decade earlier.

As part of the Khalid settlement, Prince Fahd, the leading figure of the full brother princes by a Sudeiri mother, known popularly as the 'Sudeiri Seven', became the Crown Prince.

Fahd would be the man who would take over much of the daily responsibilities of governing under Khalid. The settlement also included an entrenchment of the sharing of the kingdom's senior offices, to the balancing benefit of the rival faction to Fahd's. It was thus agreed that the leader of the non-Sudeiri faction, Prince Abdullah, would become Fahd's eventual successor, through the signalling device of making him second deputy prime minister. Thus was balance preserved among the senior clan members, and the issue of the succession but one settled well in advance of its necessity.

Kuwait too was convulsed by leadership struggles at the end of the nineteenth century, when Amir Mubarak (later known as 'the Great'), ensured his rule by killing two of his brothers and usurping the throne. A period of domestic despotism followed until Mubarak's death in 1915, a softening of authority following thereafter, especially under the long rule of Ahmad al-Jaber. His successor, Abdullah al-Salim (1950–65), in particular was known for delegating governmental powers through the Sabah family as the complexity of government increased. In 1959 he called on his nephew, Sheikh Jaber al-Ahmad, to take over the management of the emirate's finances, thereby helping to signify the importance of the man who would become Amir once the succession passed to the next generation.

The negotiated nature of this type of leadership helps define the style and conduct of such leadership when in office. The involvement of multiple actors rather than a dominant figure gives a greater sense of shared leadership. While the king is certainly first among equals in Saudi Arabia, the concept of the collective consultation of the important senior princes has emerged since the death of Abdul Aziz. This has been the case during moments of national crisis, such as when Riyadh debated whether or not to invite American troops into the kingdom to deter a possible Iraqi invasion during the Kuwait crisis in 1990. In Kuwait a greater spirit of broad-based leadership may be seen in the distribution of cabinet portfolios to senior Sabah family members. The existence of a partially elected National Assembly, established in its infancy in 1938, is an institutional expression of a broader commitment to scrutiny and account-ability. Though there is a hurly burly quality to such domestic politics – successive emirs dissolved the assembly in 1976 and 1986 such was their frustration with the stubborn independent-mindedness of it – Kuwait has taken on an institutionalised process of semi-democratic incorporation as a result.

In terms of mass based relations, Kuwait benefits from being a more sophisticated entity than is the case elsewhere in the Gulf, with a relatively free press, a lively and intellectually vigor-ous university and an informal but nevertheless efficient process whereby news and views are communicated and discussed through the emirate. The latter, known as the *diwaniyya* system, involves a series of overlapping private hierarchical forums that provides an effective form of political communication between the upper and lower echelons of the citizenry, even embracing members of the ruling family at the top. There is also a parallel system for women in the emirate. This provides the ruling family with the opportunity to take better informed and trialled decisions, though it of course provides no guarantees of wise outcomes.

The conduct of government under such figures has condi-tioned the context under which the political succession has taken place. This is the case informally but also increasingly formally in the region. In Saudi Arabia an informal concave of the senior princes has been used in the past to endorse the next king. A family council has been announced to take over the task in the future; it is expected that this will be the device used both to endorse Prince Sultan, the kingdom's current heir apparent, and to nominate his successor when King Abdullah passes away. In Kuwait in January 2006 the National Assembly helped to overturn the old intra-Sabah accord between the al-Ahmad and al-Salim branches of the ruling family, a reflection of the old intra-regime balance proving to be no longer viable. This reality was epitomised by the senility of the only candidate of senior standing of the al-Salim branch, Shaikh Saad. After the briefest of interludes, the succession subsequently passed to Shaikh Sabah, the former foreign minister, and member of the al-Ahmad branch, who had latterly become the country's prime minister, in the face of Saad's incapacitation. The Amir Sabah subsequently appointed two other members of his line to be the prime minister and heir apparent. There were younger al-Salim branch members included in the new cabinet, but at a much lower rank. Under the latest accommodation the al-Salim branch had been reduced, as the meritocratic nature of the original understanding proved to be no longer sustainable, and it had been achieved in an orderly and effective way.

The institutional leader

The fourth type of leadership to be found in the Middle East is the institutional leader, that is to say the leader who emerges from and whose standing is closely associated with the dominant institutions of the state. Its variants may be: a military junta that seizes power; a military hierarchy that wields political power indirectly from its institutional base; retired military officers who become politicians after retirement; members of a strong civilian institution, who exercise substantive political power. A strong parallel from elsewhere in the developing world would include successive presidents of Mexico prior to 2000; the nominations of the Institutional Revolutionary Party (PRI), they retire into relative obscurity after a single term in office. Military rulers at different times in Pakistan would also qualify. Examples from the Middle East would include: major figures from sundry revolutionary institutions in Iran since 1979; important Turkish military leaders whether at times of direct (e.g. Kenan Evren the leader of the September 1980 takeover) or indirect interventions (e.g. Ismail Hakki Karadayi in 1997); senior Israeli generals (Dayan, Rabin, Sharon, Barak) who later enjoyed high achieving political careers, at first because of the prominence they had enjoyed in their prior professional life stemming from long service in the military.

In this case the successful leader owes little to personal attributes alone, whether charismatic or manufactured, or to the negotiations among small groups of personalities. Instead, it is the institutional affiliation and the opportunity that this membership gives to establish credentials that is important. The actual leader is identified as an institutional man rather than as a strong man. In the case of the Turkish military, the successful leader is moulded from the age of fourteen, having been plucked from social obscurity, on the basis of individual promise. A great honour for people of modest backgrounds, he will then attend a military high school, before undergoing officer training. If tipped for the top, he will spend at least one stint in the relevant Turkish staff college. Because of Turkey's membership of Nato, there are many opportunities for training courses and substantive postings abroad, notably to the US, Germany and Nato headquarters in Brussels. In Israel, it is the achievements made with the military, which have brought men who would become leading politicians to the attention of the general public. This may be as a result of a significant role played in a decisive military victory. Moshe Dayan's battlefield success in the Sinai campaign in 1956 was the best instance of this. Yitzhak Rabin was another politician to benefit from sweeping military success, in his case having been chief of staff during the victory of the June 1967 war.

In all cases, the institutional association confers great authority on the individual leader or leaders, especially in relation to other sources of elite standing. As has been demonstrated on numerous occasions, at least up to 2002, it is very difficult for civilian politicians in Turkey openly to contradict or oppose the country's senior military commanders. When on 28 February 1997, during Turkey's infamous 'post-modern coup', the military submitted its list of demands to the then Islamist prime minister, Necmettin Erbakan, rather than defiantly resist such a challenge on democratic grounds, he meekly accepted the process. In Turkey it is important to emphasise that it is the position rather than the personality that decisively counts. When the high profile and unusually voluable deputy chief of staff, Cevik Bir, sought a political career after retirement in 1999 he was regarded as having overstepped the mark. Once he had stepped down, he was shunned by his former military peers. He was also ridiculed in the national press, it is presumed with the connivance of his former colleagues. When Israel invaded Lebanon in 1982, the decision and its implementation was driven forward by the defence minister, Ariel Sharon, supported by the right wing chief of staff, Raphael Eitan. Though the prime minister Menachem Begin was the third member of the triumvirate prosecuting the war, he was by far the least experienced in warfare. As such, he was a rather hapless figurehead for what in the end became not only a risky enterprise but ultimately a self-defeating one. Once the disastrous nature of the 1982 invasion had become clear, Begin soon after left politics for a remaining life of seclusion and mourning.

The backing of a strong institution is invariably a boon for leadership more widely. In public opinion surveys in Turkey the military is regularly identified as the institution inspiring the greatest respect in society. This has echoes of the old Ottoman expectation that the individual exists to serve the state (rather than its more familiar liberal inversion). Shimon Peres was persistently viewed as an unreliable peace-maker, even after forty years in politics, in part because he had no CV of high military achievement. Peres was regarded as a somewhat slippery and untrustworthy figure, cutting deals in smoke-filled rooms, in contrast to the simple but noble conception of the career military officer as upright and straightforward. Binyamin Netanyahu, with only a short career in the military to his credit, closely associated himself with his brother Yonatan, a special forces commando and Israel's only fatality during the raid on Entebbe in 1976 to free hostages from a hijacked civilian aircraft. Meanwhile, everyone in Israel is aware that former premier Ehud Barak, the current leader of the Labour Party, is also the country's most decorated former general.

In policy terms, both Turks and Israelis undoubtedly continue to be highly influenced by the defence establishments in both countries. Both have strong military industrial sectors. In Turkey the top commanders have always reserved the right to express their views on security matters through the institution of the National Security Council, a body chaired by the president and comprising both generals and ministers. In Turkey many areas of policy have been securitised, including such less obvious fields as education and energy matters. With its institutional cohesion and its shared values of Kemalism, the military has until recently usually prevailed in the development of key areas of policy. In Israel the general-cum-politician only becomes a politician after he has retired from the military (with an additional distancing period). Even here, of course, the main networks of the retired commander will be largely defence in orientation. On becoming prime minister in 1999, Ehud Barak famously, and unwisely, created a 'kitchen cabinet' comprised extensively of retired generals. Clearly he only trusted men like himself, especially in the murky field of government.

With strong institutions and the intervening process of elections, as volatile and unpredictable almost as anywhere, it is difficult for serving politicians to micro-manage the political succession. Military promotions are the exclusive domain of the serving military in Israel, as they are in Turkey, in spite of the head of government chairing the promotions panel. In Turkey, the generals that have become drawn into the process of government have usually been quick to step down. In 1997, Karadayi handed over the position of chief of staff when his time had elapsed, and has retained no national political profile since. General Evren managed to prolong his position in politics after the 1980 full-blooded military coup, by getting himself chosen as president. Once government had been handed back to the civilians through a democratic process, authority drained away from Evren and he finished his term as little more than an old man in the garb of office.

In Israel, the political parties eye the rising chiefs of staff with a view to their political recruitment. Figures such as Barak were a big catch. Like Eisenhower in the US in the early 1950s, Barak could probably have had his choice of parties. On occasion, the retiring chief proves not to be capable of holding his own in the bruising chaos of civilian politics in Israel, where values such as hierarchy and respect have long broken down. Amnon Lipkin Shahak, though a success as the country's top soldier, failed to entrench the newly created Centre Party in the 1999 election. Sometimes, the chief has a specific ideological vision of their own that they wish to propagate. Raphael Eitan eschewed the existing range of political parties in favour of the creation of his own rightist party, a group that prospered around his personality, and was largely based on those who had served under him.

In the Middle East leadership matters. In the absence of embedded institutions and a tradition of the division of powers, the peoples of the region tend to look to their leaders to stamp their authority upon the political process. This can easily lead to demagoguery. The sense of expectation that this elicited was greater in the 1950s and 1960s, when Middle Eastern societies had high levels of belief in politics as a vehicle for the transformation of society. Nasser was the epitome of the leader who expressed the collective emotional aspiration for change. It was in the Gulf states, where oil fortuitously impacted small economies, that leaders like Shaikh Zayed in Abu Dhabi made less noise but could claim the better record.

Since that time, people's idealised expectations of their leaders have been punctured. Political regimes are now more complex; their ouster more difficult because of broader coalitions of power and the presence of multiple security agencies. This has even been the case in the democracies of the Middle East, where successive Israeli premiers and presidents of late have been mired in corruption allegations and accusations of sexual misconduct. As in ancient Rome, the mob (or 'street' in the modern Middle East) remains a significant actor, expectant and capable of mobilisation. But it is also a fickle participant, ready to treat those it deems a success with adulation and an unctuous deference; for those that are perceived as failures, it is largely contemptuous and unforgiving.

8
Society

One hundred years ago and the dominant themes of Middle Eastern society would probably have been rural, passive and slow paced in nature. The peasant (*fellah*) tilling the field using an ox plough. Personal comfort derived from simple pleasures, such as drinking sweet, black tea and playing backgammon in a Spartan cafe. The governor (*vali*) and the Islamic justice (*qadi*) as the main authority figures in the area. Widespread illiteracy in the absence of state education. Quakish and ineffectual remedies for ill health. The village as the economic and social focal point.

Today, while many of the tastes of the region remain the same (sweet, black tea most notably), the pace and focus of life has been transformed. Middle East society in the early twenty-first century is predominantly an active, faster-paced, more urban experience. It takes place in sprawling conurbations, teeming with children, and with loud, middle aged women. Extended families live on top of each other in new floors constructed for the purpose. It is noisy, with the sound of every size of motor vehicle, the larger ones belching smoky fumes. The presence of the state is closer, especially its extensive networks of shadowy secret police. But life expectancy has risen and there is state provided education. Television, soap operas and cheap videos dominate popular culture and provide an escape from the grind of modern life.

Birth

The most tangible way that Middle Eastern society has been transformed is in the sheer numbers of people that now populate it. This is the case for Arabs, Iranians, Kurds, Orthodox Jews and Turks alike. In 1950, according to the UN, there were just 104 million people in the region. By 2007 that figure had grown to 432 million. Projecting this growth forward would leave the region with a population of 692 million in 2050. Helping to generate this increase has been natural population growth from the 1970s through the 1990s of between 3.5% and 4% per annum. At times, the natural growth rate has nudged the highest levels possible. Tunisia is the only Arab country in the region that does not conform to this pattern of rampant population growth. As a result, a stunning statistic holds sway for most of the region: 60% of the population is under the age of 24.

Lauded as a gift from God, and celebrated as the region's greatest resource, elites and masses alike looked favourably on the upsurge in population growth. In reality this was a naive and short-term reaction. The baby boom triggered a big upsurge in demand for public services. In some cases, such as housing, people had no choice but to cope by sleeping more of their children in a room. In other areas there was no way of disguising demand, for instance in the education sector. Shortages of schools and classrooms have been major constraints, at all levels. Secondary schools were obliged to operate on a double shift basis in many parts of the region. The surge in demand did not allow state schools the time or the resources to develop the curriculum. Pedagogy remained primitive in its approach, with rote learning a technique of choice. The acute strain on resources has allowed large numbers of children to fall through the educational net, notably girls. The Middle East countries have generally lagged behind other regions of the developing world in terms of the quality of education.

As the baby bulge has fed through the system, other areas have found themselves under pressure. This includes the higher education sector, which has undergone a major expansion over the last thirty years. New universities were created and existing ones expanded. While many of the former were presented as institutions of science and technology, doubts existed about the level of resourcing and the size of the intake. There are other difficulties. In Arab universities it is very difficult for academics to fail their students because of the social pressure that can be brought to bear. In existing institutions, expansion was hardly financed properly. Where it was, these resources were often diverted to soft subject areas. In Saudi Arabia, this meant departments of Islamic affairs, controlled by the kingdom's religious hierarchy. An increasing number of younger Saudis have subsequently graduated from such departments without adequate preparation for joining the national labour pool, which craves practical subjects.

The expansion in tertiary education has also seen the creation of a range of vocational and community colleges. There have been severe doubts about the quality of the specialist skills on offer. This is exacerbated by the social stigma associated with blue collar technical skills and service sector work, such as waiting at table, especially in the Gulf states. Many of these institutions (and some of the new universities) are privately owned, with question marks over the ability of the state to regulate such a rapidly growing area.

The old traditions and their durability

If the Middle East has undergone many transformations over the last century, some of its old practices and values have proved to be flexible, adaptable and enduring. At the forefront of these has been the practice of kin group solidarity that tends to be conflated into the catchall term of 'tribalism'. In a phrase, tribalism is a system of collective security that provides safety in numbers. The fact that an individual can look for help and safety to an extended family and, beyond that, to an extended clan (real, imagined or created, e.g. through marriage) means that tribalism is a great supplier of security, both economic and physical, to that individual.

A hypothetical case serves to illustrate. The shepherd with his flock on an isolated hillside has less to fear in a tribal system than he would if he were merely an individual. Anyone seeking to exploit, hurt or expropriate him would be deterred from doing so by the existence of tribal solidarity. This solidarity is based on an 'all for one and one for all' mentality ('*asabiya*). If for some reason the potential attacker failed to be deterred and went ahead with a violation, the dispute would take on a corporatist nature: the aggressor would have to be prepared for the retribution of the shepherd's tribe. Moreover, this retaliation could be directed at any one of the violator tribe's number, to ensure against the frustration of the individual perpetrator being spirited away or closely defended. The corporatist nature of the dispute would mean that the most senior member of the tribe or, at the other end of the spectrum, the youngest of juveniles within the tribe could be the target for retaliation, because young and old, junior and senior, all carry the tribe's metaphorical mark.

In theory, the consequence of such a corporatist escalation would be an indefinite tribal vendetta, reminiscent of parts of the Balkans like Albania. In practice, third party mediation (the head of a disinterested tribe or perhaps a senior state official) would almost certainly be mobilised, and the dispute settled through negotiation, with appropriate compensation ('blood money' to cover loss of earnings in the case of a killing) being rendered to the injured party or their dependents.

This tribal system worked well enough in the past on the margins of empire, where state authority was theoretical rather than practical. The establishment of a modern state system in the region from the 1920s might have been expected to end the practice. After all, what was the liberal state for if not to protect its members from external attack and regulate the affairs of its citizens within? In practice, however, it was not a system of liberal states that was established in the Middle East. The states were themselves often a reflection of dominant kin groups such as in Saudi Arabia (where the dominant clan of 'Saud' have had themselves written into the very geography of the land) and the Gulf states, rather than a set of institutions functioning above all such parochial divisions. The so-called radical states of the region too came to reflect narrow ethnic, sectarian and tribal interests, such as in Iraq and Syria, where those partial interests had captured the state through a military takeover. The recourse to formal legal mechanisms was in any case notoriously slow and bureaucratic. Rather than fading away or becoming anachronistic, individuals continued to see value in tribal solidarity, as a way of ensuring protection from the state, or as a vehicle through which to unlock the resources and benefits of the state.

Tribalism is alive and vigorous in the contemporary Middle East. In some parts of the region, notably Iraq given the abject insecurity of the country since 2003, tribal solidarity is still invoked for existential reasons of physical security. This has been particularly evident in Sunni Arab Iraq, where tribal solidarity forms the basis of the 'Awakening Councils', the paramilitary formations funded by the US in the west and north-west of the country since 2006.

In a modern setting tribalism's real value lies in an informal though embedded system of intercession (*wasta*), the benefits that its mediation delivers to individuals who would be relatively powerless were they to have to function on their own. A good example of tribalism in action today may be seen in the search for jobs in a region where unemployment has risen precipitately and a torrent of young people are coming onto the jobs market each year. If one visits parliaments across the region (Turkey and Iran, as well as the Arab world), one is struck by the number of constituents who have come to see their MPs. A reflection of lively constituency politics in a representational democratic system with traction? No, just people trying to beg and cajole MPs to find work for their fellow clan members.

While tribalism is a boon for many in the region it is not a resource that all have access to equally. Those who have been socially damaged are less likely to be able to mobilise tribal resources on their behalf. Such categories would include: the family headed by a female after the early death of a patriarch; those identified as marginals (e.g. gypsies); families dishonoured

TRIBAL CULTURE

Tribes have relatively flat as opposed to steep hierarchies of power. Individual tribesmen tend to be able to gain direct access to the headman (*sheikh*), a sign that the latter cares about the well-being of the former. The tribesman may well address the head through a respectful familiarity, notably by addressing him as the father of his eldest son (in my case Abu Edmund). The quality of the tribal leadership is judged by the way in which such petitions are dealt with and the ability of the authority figure to bring about satisfactory outcomes. The criteria for choosing a new tribal head is usually a combination of two things. First, high birth; other than in a context of complete turmoil the head needs to be able to draw on the nobility of his birth. This shaikhly genealogical line allows the new leader to assert an authority, accumulated and bolstered over generations. Second, ability; there is no point in having a leader if he has no meritocratic qualities. Thus, succession within the tribe is not necessarily based on primogeniture; younger brother or cousin successions (sometimes disputed) are possible. Once a new head is chosen, he must continue to prove himself as being fit for the role. This can be done through the wisdom that comes with good and successful decisions. It must also be done through culturally appropriate behaviour. He must be a person who takes such values as hospitality and generosity seriously (*karim*). There must be respect for the elderly. Local disputes are settled through the application of tribal law, a non-codified common law, the corpus of which is retained by tribes through an oral tradition.

(e.g. through illegitimacy or for actual or perceived involvement in prostitution). Moreover, the further one is located from the seat of power, whether geographically, economically or socially, the more difficult it is to access elite networks, if only as a humble supplicant. In general, poor, rural families without the benefit of extensive clan relations or any claim to social standing are the ones that are most likely to lose out under a tribal system.

HOSPITALITY

The Middle East and especially the Arab world has a deserved reputation for warmth and hospitality. Such phrases as 'you are welcome' (*ahlan wa sahlan*) and 'my house is your house' (*bayti baytak*) are familiar ones that feature early on in exchanges between the newly introduced. The act of touching one's heart after a handshake to denote sincerity is an arresting one. Middle Eastern men when meeting usually supplement the handshake with the kissing of the cheeks and an embrace in order to underline the warmth of the relationship. Hospitality often extends to the sharing of meals, traditionally in single sex gatherings in the home or as part of public ceremonies, such as the breaking of the fast (*iftar*) during Ramadan, the month of fasting. Increasingly, entertaining is undertaken in restaurants. The older generation frowned on restaurant dining: it generated pity for those who clearly had no home to go to! Today, the restaurant has probably supplanted the home as a venue at which to entertain, especially for the well to do. In an expensive restaurant one can display one's wealth, and by implication one's power. One can also show off one's guests, especially if they have a high local status, or are foreign business-men, diplomats or journalists. The key to any successful lunch or dinner is generosity. There must be more dishes, both the multiple individual starter dishes (*mezze*) and the meat-based main courses (usually the ubiquitous kebabs) than any guest can hope to consume. Such generosity confers honour upon both host and guest, the former as a reflection of his wealth and his attentiveness, the latter because of the spread that his standing has merited.

The sport of kings

Sporting prowess has long been recognised and valued in the region, even though its outlets have been limited. Historically, it was the sports of the saddle that would have been most highly prized. For Bedouin tribes, the ability to harness and utilise camel transport was a necessity of a mobile life in areas of marginal ecology. The skills of the rider were deployed recreationally, notably in the form of camel racing. Today, camel racing has become a major seasonal sport in the UAE and big business too. Controversy has dogged the sport in recent times owing to allegations of the abduction and virtual enslavement of young boys as racing jockeys.

For the elites of the day, horsemanship was regarded as a pastime commensurate with their status. This has continued into contemporary times, through patronage of the sport of horse racing, notably by the Maktoums, the ruling family of the emirate of Dubai, and in particular the current ruler of the emirate, Shaikh Muhammad bin Rashid al-Maktoum. He has the largest stake in his family owned Godolphin stables in England. Shaikh Muhammad hosts the richest series of horse races in the world, in the form of the Dubai World Cup.

Not all Arab elites have vacated the saddle in exchange for a more passive role as patron. Basel al-Asad, the eldest son and presumed favoured successor (before his untimely death) of President Asad of Syria, made a considerable name for himself as a show jumper at international tournaments. Part macho male, part celebrity, Basel's prowess on a horse was a device through which to demonstrate his physical strength and mental alertness, both components of a fitness for ruling. A number of the offspring of Shaikh Muhammad have recently met with comparable success. Four of his sons were successful winners of gold endurance racing medals at the 15th Asian Games in 2006, and his daughter was placed in the show jumping competition.

The Hashemites of Jordan have long taken an interest in breeding the coveted Arabian thoroughbred horses, showing them off and entering them in competition. King Hussein's eldest child, Princess Alia, is the director of the royal stables. It was his fourth daughter (and sixth child), Princess Haya, who was the international competitor in the family, entering the 2000 Sydney Olympics as a show jumper, and even carrying the Jordanian flag during the ceremonial march past of country teams. She subsequently married Shaikh Muhammad, the ruler of Dubai in 2004, in a match made in an equine heaven, and is delicately referred to as his 'junior', that is to say his second and concurrent, wife. Haya enjoyed international success as the owner of the 2008 Epsom Derby winner, New Approach, a gift to her from her husband.

The sport of youth

If saddle sports have been the sports of kings and their ilk, soccer has emerged over the last three decades as the uncontested sport of the masses. With the demographic profile of the region being dominated by the young, this means the sport of youth *(shebab)*. Soccer is mainly played rather than watched live in the region. Professional teams have been modest in their achievement hitherto. Middle Eastern youth would rather watch the world famous teams of Britain, Italy and Spain, and are keen consumers of the merchandising of the likes of Manchester United, Liverpool, Real Madrid and Inter Milan. Soccer is a sport that can be played in the street, a mode of play that is unconsciously loyal to the origins of the game in working class England in the nineteenth century. It can also be played in the various 'sports cities' *(medinat al-riyadiyat)* to be found across the Arab world, ageing centres from the period of the expansion of sporting complexes, some early fruit of the first oil boom in the 1970s.

Each individual country in the region has its own soccer administration and its own national league system. Usually each country only has two or three teams of enduring stature, a reflection of the shortage of money and talent in the national game. While the rivalry between these elite clubs may be intense and continuing, the rest of the league lags well behind, making the outcome of most games tediously predictable.

The national league in Turkey arguably achieves the highest standard, mainly because Turkey is actually part of the Union of European Football Associations (UEFA). As a result, leading Turkish clubs participate in Europe's annual Champions League and the UEFA cup competition. The playing company of Europe's top clubs has forced up the standards in Turkey. A share of the television rights has given Turkey's top four clubs – Besiktas, Fenerbahce, Galatasaray and, the only non-Istanbul based team among the elite, Trabzonspor – something of the buying power of Europe's best, enabling them to at least be competitive. A smattering of the world's elite players and coaches have ended up spending usually short spells of time at Turkish clubs. In Fatih Terim, Turkey has produced at least one coach who can hold his own in the European club system. In 2000 a Turkish club side, Galatasaray, won the UEFA Cup defeating Arsenal in the final, the first and hitherto only such success by a Turkish club.

There has also been the soccer equivalent of a brain drain to some of the better known teams in Europe. Again, Turkey, together with Israel, is the most frequent source, with players such as Tuncay Sanli, Tuguy Kerimoglu and Emre Belozoglu playing in the English Premiership. Israeli players have been a small but regular feature of the English league for a couple of decades, since the days of the redoubtable Ronnie Rosenthal playing for Liverpool. Of course there are many players of Arab origin playing in Europe, of whom the most famous and feted was Zinedene Zidane. Though Berber Algerian in origin,

Zidane was born and raised in France and went on to play for the national team, featuring in the World Cup winning side of 1998 and the successful Euro 2000 side two years later. The loss of such potential players as a by-product of labour migration to the European continent is a galling reality for many countries on the southern side of the Mediterranean rim.

In the same way that some European clubs are still associated with the primordial affiliations of the past (e.g. the confessionalism of Celtic and Rangers in Scotland), primordial associations have attached themselves to certain teams in the current national setup in the region. In Jordan, for example, the Faisali club, run by the Adwan clan, is strongly associated with the Transjordanian East Bank of the country, and beyond it the military elite. Their main rival, Wihdat, bearing the same name as one of Amman's largest Palestinian refugee camps, is strongly associated with Palestinian nationalism. In the 1980s growing violence at and after matches between the two clubs led the authorities to intervene, for fear that the tensions might spill over into sustained street violence. As a result, the Wihdat board stood down and the club's name was changed to al-Daffatayn (the two banks), an attempt to reflect both the Palestinian and Transjordanian aspects of the country rather than its national division. With the change proving unpopular among the team's supporters, but with the violence ended, Wihdat was quietly given its old name back a couple of years later.

Primordialism is very much alive in Israeli soccer too, with the football clubs taking 'Hapoel' as their prefix coming from a labour/trade union background, while the origins of 'Betar' teams is the Revisionist Zionism of the right wing Jewish activist of the 1920s and 1930s, Vladimir Jabotinsky. Followers of Betar Jerusalem, one of Israel's more successful sides, are infamously politically incorrect in their attitude towards and treatment of Arab players, for instance through terrace chanting. By contrast, the small club of Sakhnin has emerged in the 2000s as a symbol of hope, not only of Jews and Arabs playing together in a mixed team, but as a wider symbol of inter-communal cooperation. In 2004 Sakhnin won the Israeli knock-out cup, giving the club a profile and an impact disproportionate to its size. The club home, the Doha Stadium, was funded by Qatar, an arresting and rarely publicised example of Arab investment in Israel.

A VISIT TO THE FREEDOM STADIUM

Iran's main soccer venue is the Freedom (*Azadi*) Stadium, where international and big club matches are played. The latter usually feature at least one of the country's two main teams, Persepolis (after the ancient capital), and Crown (*taj*). Neither are formally called by those names, the connections with Iran's ancient monarchy being too discomforting for the ruling regime. Most Iranian football fans insist on using the old names, as a matter of tradition, and also to annoy their political masters. The grave looking and bearded photographs of the Supreme Leader, Ayatollah Khomeini, and his successor, Ali Khamenei, stare down at the pitch from the roof of the stadium, resulting in the oft repeated quip that they are Iran's greatest football fans, as they never miss a game. Big games also attract a large security presence, with secret police patrolling the touchlines, guns under their shirts. After the match the spirit of exuberance takes a little time to dissipate. Such feelings find an outlet in the honking of car horns, the chanting of club and player names and largely good natured abuse directed towards the opposition fans in other vehicles.

As in Europe, the national teams of the Middle East have increasingly come to represent the collective aspirations of the people on the international stage. As at club level, the principal example is Turkey, which has achieved a level of success on a Euro-continental and global level since the 1980s unseen in the rest of the region. In 2002, Turkey won the play-off game to take third place in the World Cup hosted by Japan and South Korea. Turkey is now a regular qualifier for World Cup and European Championships, whereas regional participation in the former is invariably limited. A second example is the Iraq national team, which won the 2007 Asian Cup, beating Saudi Arabia in the final, just three years after undergoing the trauma of war and regime change. Under the previous regime, the national squad had been regularly abused by Saddam Hussein's sadistic eldest son, Uday, who curried favour with the Iraqi young by, among other things, serving as the president of the country's football federation. Significant regional success has also been posted in the African Cup of Nations, where Egypt has won the biennial trophy a record six times, including back to back wins in 2006 and 2008. Algeria, Morocco, Sudan and Tunisia from the Middle East have also won the cup.

Alongside soccer, interest in other sports pales. There is a growing following for basketball, with Turkey and Israel high aspirants. A range of minority sports, like volleyball, have their followers. The other sport where significant achievements have been posted is in men's middle distance running in Arab North Africa, where success has become something of a regularity for Morocco and Tunisia. Mohammed Gammoudi won four Olympic running medals for Tunisia between 1964 and 1972. Egypt has proved to be the Arab world's most prolific performer in summer Olympics with a total of twenty-four medals, just ahead of Morocco with twenty-one, though the latter can boast some of the best known Olympians, notably Said Aouita (5000 m gold, 1984) and Hicham El-Guerrouj (1500 m & 5000 m golds, 2004). Arab countries have won seventy-three medals in a century of Olympic competition. At the 2008 Beijing Olympics, Turkey came thirty-seventh in the medals table, Iran fifty-first, Bahrain fifty-second and Tunisia fifty-fifth.

Youth culture

The tastes, attitudes and mores of the region's young is a topic of earnest discussion, comparable to debates about the outlook of its likely future political affiliations. Much is at stake; from the businessmen that seek to anticipate shifts in the youth market, to the social conservatives, who fret about moral standards and traditional values.

Early signs are that the rising generations of the young in the region do not represent a major cultural break with the past, but are a combination of the traditional and the cautiously modern. Those brought up within culturally distinct communities with rigid social hierarchies are likely to conform to the expectations of their communities. While there are the occasional defections from groups such as the minority ultra-Orthodox Jewish communities (*haredim*) in Israel, they tend to be the exceptions that prove the rule. These communities are well organised, patriarchal, disciplined and underpinned by established rituals and norms, such as a highly distinct form of dress. The fact that the youth of these communities are exempt from military service and are financed to study at their own religious seminaries (*yeshivot*) means that there are few challenges to the prevalent world view.

In the Arab Gulf, young people are under similar social and kin pressure to conform. There is no sign that the male social uniform of the Gulf Arab – the white, floor length over garment (*thob*), red and white head-dress – is to be abandoned as the standard form of public dress, whether in favour of the business suit or the leather jacket. It is when travelling outside the Arab world that the dress codes are relaxed, much as they have been for the last couple of generations. In general, social conformity is highly prized as it is bound up with multiple layers of social re-enforcement, inevitably conservative in outlook, from the family through the clan to the neighbourhood and the religious community. Rebelling against such values and traditions is not taken lightly as a mere rite of passage as it would be in the West. Attempts to do so, where they might take place, would be treated with the utmost seriousness, rather than with a benevolent indulgence, and could involve draconian responses.

In the more mainstream communities of the wider Middle East, outside influences have been absorbed and adapted, usually with the superficiality of the passing style. Young people across most of the Arab world will largely wear Western-style dress. The sons and daughters of the well-to-do in Lebanon, regardless of their religion, are likely to collect designer labels, drink cappuccino in French-style patisseries and get married in lavish receptions in the swanky hotels of the capital. The nightclub scene is long established in the likes of Beirut, Cairo and Tel Aviv; less so across much of the rest of the region. Istanbul is just beginning to rise above its reputation for grey drabness and tackiness and is acquiring some youthfully sophisticated night life; Bodrum and Antalya have long catered for young European holidaymakers. Even 'raves' are becoming increasingly familiar events, though with a tameness that pales alongside Britain or France.

While in most parts of the region youth culture is, like its Western equivalent, primarily about having fun, there are cases where it cannot remain at the level of the frivolous. Iran is a good example. In Tehran young Iranians, fed up with the restrictiveness of the conservative social atmosphere, are making statements through their dress, actions and preferences. Attendance by young people at the various Shia religious celebrations, such as the mourning ceremonies for the iconic Shia religious martyr, Imam Hussein (*ashura*), have fallen away in number. Interest in pre-Islamic, indigenous forms of culture and religion, notably faiths such as Zoroastrianism, by contrast are booming. There is also much admiration for US culture, not least because it is frowned upon by the conservative mullahs.

Younger Iranians in the affluent suburbs of north Tehran organise clandestine showings of the latest Hollywood films. A modern favourite, *Titanic*, spawned a secondary industry in shoulder bags and T-shirts, the sheer number of which made their suppression by the authorities unfeasible. Carrying and wearing such items made them very effective 'weapons of the weak' in the passive resistance of younger people to the stultifying uniformity imposed by those in power. Other silent protests include the clothing worn by some young women under their conservative over-garments, including in some cases fishnet stockings and skirts among the shortest known to man.

The parks of north Tehran provide a neutral area where young men and women can meet up unchaperoned. On the fleeting occasions when the regime clamps down on such public mixing of the sexes, the well off tend to retreat to the mountains beyond the city, either for parties or, in the winter, for the skiing. Here alcohol is freely available, its production being permitted for use ostensibly by the country's small Armenian Christian minority. For those members of the professional middle classes for whom life simply becomes intolerable there is the ultimate option of emigration. In the poorer, more pious, southern suburbs of the city there are fewer affordable outlets through which young people may escape. A growing number of young males seek solace in the cheap heroin that has flooded the city from Afghanistan since the 1990s.

New media

Whatever the tastes and outlook of the region's young it shares with its counterpart in the West a dexterity as far as new media is concerned. Though poverty and opportunity continues to limit access to the internet to some twenty per cent of the region's population, the young are disproportionately well represented. Where regimes have sought to put crude blocks in place on the use of the internet, the young have invariably got around many of the restrictions, even in authoritarian states like Syria. Social networking sites in the region, like My Space, are becoming increasingly popular. Even Queen Rania of Jordan has launched a You Tube campaign to try to update Western conceptions of the Arab world.

An enthusiastic engagement with the opportunities offered by the new media is not in and of itself a reflection of a cosmopolitanism, a willingness to engage with the world in a positive way. Islamist terrorist organisations have successfully and chillingly mastered the new technology of the internet. Jihadi websites have been used effectively to promote recruit-ment. An example was the Istanbul bombers of 2003, who targeted Jewish and British commercial interests in the city after having been radicalised in the internet cafes of south-eastern Turkey. This has been done by showing repeated images of radical Muslims undergoing military training, and images of attacks on their targets of choice, whether Israeli settlers in Palestine or American troops in Iraq. The message seems to be one of empowerment, urging Muslims to shrug off external domination in favour of direct and effective action. Such websites have also carried the unedifying images of beheadings, usually of Western civilians unlucky enough to have been caught up in the struggle for power in Iraq.

For most younger people in the region new media equates with little more than breadth of entertainment and the opportu-nity to access news with a different narrative from that which their own political regime broadcasts to them. In Iran, the enthusiasm for new media has arguably eclipsed that of anywhere else in the region with satellite dishes installed across the capital even when doing so had been declared to be illegal. This in part reflects the relative political sophistication of the Iranians. In part it reflects the large and politically active Iranian diaspora, many of whom are implacable opponents of the ruling regime. With over one million expatriate Iranians living in California, they are the Middle East equivalent of America's Cuban exiles in Florida. It is their invective that most intensively challenges the view from Tehran.

With tens of television channels available across the Middle East, the outcome has not so much been pluralism as fragmentation. It now seems laughable to look back on the aversion that

FRUSTRATION AND ACQUIESCENCE IN SYRIA

With its authoritarian regime and state dominated economy, Syria has all of the attractions of the former Soviet Union on a bad day. As elsewhere in the region, one of the people's most effective coping mechanisms is humour. One joke, a perennial favourite, goes thus:

Every day there is a long queue outside the neighbourhood bakery for bread. One day a well-known figure in the area breaks with the frustration of it all. 'That's it,' he exclaims, 'I've had enough! I'm going to the presidential palace to kill Asad.' Next day the queue has formed outside the same bakery when the people see the same man meekly come and join the queue. 'What happened?' demanded the crowd. 'We thought you were going to the presidential palace to kill Asad.' 'I did go to the presidential palace,' the man weakly protested. 'But there was a queue!'

On another occasion I was walking with a Syrian friend in central Damascus in the late 1990s. The traffic was roaring along at great speed. We were having to step on and off the curb because of a large number of vehicles parked on the pavement, thereby putting our lives in jeopardy every time. 'I want to form an association to campaign against cars parking on the pavement,' my friend suddenly erupted in frustration. 'That's a good idea,' I said encouragingly. 'It would never be allowed,' he said. 'In the absence of any associations independent of regime and state, it would become politicised overnight, and I would be in big trouble.'

regimes had for new technologies in the region. In the 1980s Damascus feared the fax machine; in the 1990s it feared the internet. In neither case did it need to do so, and both, after a long period of proscription, are now permitted. The one exception is the al-Jazeera phenomenon, the Arab satellite station broadcasting from Qatar. Over the first decade of its existence, al-Jazeera displayed innovation and dynamism in a region that had acquired a reputation for safe and deferential broadcasting. Its viewing figures were said to top forty million. Through its live debates and stark images of Iraqis and Palestinians living under occupation, al-Jazeera gained a regional following, especially among Arab intellectuals, who lapped up the transmissions with a righteous sense of outrage. In the last couple of years, however, the satellite station has lost at least some of its lustre, even as it has diversified into English language transmission. It has fallen foul of three things. One, competition from rivals, such as al-Arabiya, cloned and resourced by rival emirates elsewhere in the Gulf. Two, the realisation that al-Jazeera broadcasts critical programmes on all countries of the region, with the exception of its host country, thereby helping to dilute its reputation for fearless journalism and expose a certain sanctimoniousness of attitude. More recently, the Doha government has shackled the station in its reporting of Saudi Arabia, a part of the rapprochement package negotiated between these erstwhile enemies. Three, suspicions that al-Jazeera was sometimes too quick to get to a story, especially where it involved violent protest or insurgency attacks, suggesting that the station might have been a little too closely associated with radical elements in the region.

Death

According to Muslim tradition, the dead should be buried on

the same day as their passing. The body should be cleaned and wrapped in a simple white shroud. In origin presumably a matter of practicality to prevent putrification, the practice has now entered the realm of embedded cultural and religious practice. Death is generally regarded as the moment that the soul leaves the body. Excessive demonstrations of grief are discouraged as this might imply doubt in the soul's continued existence after death.

Attitudes to the dead differ somewhat across the region. In Saudi Arabia, with its root and branch Wahhabism, best practice is unambiguous. There should be no question of the worship of the dead. This translates into even King Fahd having been buried in an unmarked grave following his simple funeral in 2005. Indeed, even the founder of the religious movement itself is buried in a modest site, which is ill kept. Wahhabism frowns especially hard on the sufi practice of revering saints and conducting pilgrimages to their burial places in order to seek their blessedness (*baraka*).

By contrast, the death of the Iranian Supreme Leader, Ayatollah Khomeini, in June 1989 led to tumultuous scenes. An estimated eleven million people joined the throng to pay their respects. As the funeral party made its way towards the burial place there were outpourings of grief that only a Shia crowd would know how to generate. At one stage, as the hysteria rose in intensity, Khomeini's body was almost lost in the crowd, as mourners tried to grab pieces of the shroud as religious relics. Khomeini was eventually buried at the second attempt in a mausoleum in the southern part of the city, close to Tehran's largest cemetery, The Paradise of Zahra (*Behesht-e Zahra*), where many of the 'martyrs' of the Iran–Iraq war had been laid to rest. In time, the mausoleum has been expanded into a large complex, including a seminary, an Islamic university, a shopping mall and a 20,000 space car park. When finally complete, it will cover some 20 sq km. Having given him a rousing send off, the

Islamic regime has bestowed upon Khomeini a standing in death commensurate with his place as the founding father of the revolution.

Society in the Middle East is as rich and diversified as the states of the region are regimented, inflexible and partial. This reflects the composition of societies in the region, notably with their large youth component. The passions of global popular culture, music and football, are as keenly embraced as they are anywhere in the world. Television is the opium of these masses today. Family life is central to the well-being of its people in terms of creating a secure atmosphere in which children can grow. Tribalism has proved to be resilient in remaining relevant to people, notably in providing access to benefits, and social safety nets for the less fortunate in adulthood. As to that crucial benchmark of secure neighbourhoods, crime rates are generally low, by developing and developed world standards alike. Enveloping the people of the region is the Islamic religion. As we shall see, it is present at every turn, in the form of the ubiquitous mosque, the call to prayer in wrap-around sound broadcast from several minarets simultaneously, and the religiously derived names that most people carry.

9
Religion

The issue of religion has emerged as arguably the Middle East's most controversial bequest to the world. Though the region has proved to be a prolific producer of religions, it is Islam which today dominates the landscape. So ingrained is Islam in the culture, rituals and values of the contemporary Middle East that it is essentially inseparable from other regional themes. For a region where the overwhelming majority of people would identify themselves as believers, Islam is everywhere: in making sense of the past; in the anti-colonial struggle; in the moral compass of families; in a collective protest against injustice; in economic philosophy; and increasingly in the search for viable political arrangements. Given its ability to mobilise, it is not surprising that the malcontents of the region reach for the angry God of Islam to add legitimacy to their feelings or personal and sociological failings, as much as the mainstream population look to the merciful (*rahman*) and compassionate (*rahim*) God of Islam for comfort and reassurance.

In the beginning

The Middle East is the geographical source of the world's three great monotheistic religions: Judaism, Christianity and Islam. Of the big three, Judaisim and Christianity originated in historic Palestine; Islam grew up in and around two of the main cities in the province of the Hijaz, Medina and Mecca, in what is today north-western Saudi Arabia.

The size of the respective religions differs greatly. The Jewish population in the Middle East today numbers about 5.6 million, virtually all to be found in the state of Israel. Until the 1950s small but thriving Oriental Jewish communities could be found across the region, notably in Morocco, Egypt, Syria, Yemen, Iraq, Libya, Tunisia, Turkey and Iran. Since the establishment of Israel these communities have shrunk greatly or disappeared altogether, through 'pull' factor emigration to Israel and out of the region, usually for economic and security reasons. In some cases this migration has resulted from 'push' factors, notably associated with persecution in the countries of origin. Today, the most significant Jewish population in the region apart from Israel is to be found in Iran, Turkey and Tunisia.

The Middle East also enjoyed a thriving Christian population comprised of a handful of long-established churches from Chaldeans and Assyrians in Iraq, to Copts in Egypt (the origin, if one looks carefully, of the country name). There were also Maronite Catholic, Greek Orthodox and Armenian faith communities in the Levant. The list of Christian denominations grew as a result of the nineteenth- and twentieth-century missionary activities of Roman Catholicism and Protestantism, especially in places like Lebanon and southern Sudan. Indigenous Christians continue to wield a disproportionate influence in the Middle East, notably as businessmen and members of the professions (but not as top political leaders, there existing a confessional glass ceiling across the region, Lebanon excepted). But their numbers have been consistently falling as a proportion of the whole, due to lower birth rates and emigration, notably to Australia, Canada and the US. The largest Christian population in the region can be found in Egypt, where some ten per cent of a population of seventy-five million are Copts.

These trends of the last sixty years mean that increasingly the societies of the Middle East have become less cosmopolitan and pluralist. There is, for example, virtually no established Christian community resident in Pera, the old European quarter in Istanbul, the last of the city's Greek community having been largely driven out in a pogrom in September 1955. The old Levantine families have disappeared from the Mediterranean rim, notably from such cities as Alexandria, again under pressure from authoritarian regimes, driven by the exclusive political values of the ideologies of the day.

These trends mean that societies in the Middle East have become increasingly Muslim in composition. With Sunni Islam comprising some eighty-five per cent of the region's total population, there has been a growing degree of uniformity across the region. All Sunni Muslims are expected to carry out the basic requirements of the religion, the so-called 'Pillars of Islam': make the essential declaration of faith, 'there is no God but God, and Muhammad is his messenger' (*La illah illallah, Muhammad rasulallah*); pray five times a day; fast during the 'holy month' of Ramadan; pay tax for charitable and related activities (*zakat*); undertake the pilgrimage to Mecca, Medina and the other key sites at least once if able. In general, believers are also supposed to struggle in the way of God (*jihad*). This has been interpreted broadly by different traditions, from a silent inner effort to the pursuit of collective political goals. As this point shows, it would be an oversimplification to regard even Sunni Islam as monolithic. While observance of this basic template of faith is widespread, it has many local cultural variants.

The most important and visible division within Islam is between Sunnis (adherents to the 'traditions' [of the prophet]) and Shias ('the partisans' [of Imam Ali]). The division dates back to an early schism over how the succession in religious and political authority ought to move following the death of the prophet: through the four 'righteous' (*rashidun*) caliphs (Sunnis) or his descendants, notably his son-in-law and grandson, the Imams Ali and Hussein (Shias). There are also key differences within the two main branches. This reflects the fact that there is no equivalent of the Papacy in Islam, capable of authoritatively deciding and imposing an orthodoxy of belief, and supported by the force of papal supreme authority. It is therefore often problematic to make definitive statements about what is or is not permissible under Islam. Instead, an often fluid and even slightly chaotic heterogeneity exists within the religion.

In spite of the early schism, Shiism shares many of the basic tenets of Islam with Sunni Islam, especially with respect to the sanctity of the Koran, reverence for the Prophet Muhammad and adherence to the five 'pillars'. But cultural and doctrinal differences have also emerged over time. Shia ritual focuses on the two figures of Imam Ali and Imam Hussein, and in particular the sacrifices that they made through martyrdom. Imam Hussein's defeat and death at the Battle of Kerbala in southern Iraq in AD 680 is marked annually with passion plays that portray key points in the battle, and tears of grief and symbolic self-flagellation at the recall of the story. A mourning period is observed during the holy month (*muharrem*) culminating in the climax of the forty day period (*arba'in*). In its rituals, Shiism is closer to Catholicism, with its personalised reverence for key religious leaders or Imams. People are more free to follow and pay their religious taxes to whichever senior person of religious learning (*marja'-e taqlid*) seems most deserving. In Sunni Islam (more akin in its public displays to nonconformist Protestantism) there are four schools of jurisprudence, and a handful of religious centres of note, of which al-Azhar University in Cairo is the oldest.

More generally, the Muslim World is a spiritually pluralist place. This is best epitomised by the presence at any one time of a number of Sufi movements. Sufism is a practice exclusive to Sunni Islam. It came on the scene around the ninth and tenth centuries. These often colourful figures, propagate a diverse and mystical approach to religion. The 'Whirling Dervishes' of central Anatolia are probably the Sufis most familiar to a Western audience. This order uses music and continuous circular movement in order to promote a higher plane of religious consciousness. Some of these orders, such as the Naqsibendi and Sanussi, developed into organised networks reminiscent to a Western eye of freemasonry in terms of their reach and extra-religious functions.

The broadly sequential nature of the three religions – Judaism, Christianity, Islam – means that they have rather differing attitudes to one another. For traditional religious Judaism, a non-evangelical religion, the wait continues for the Messiah, with all subsequent elaborations of faith essentially irrelevant. Christianity and its mainstream denominations are based firmly on the Judaic tradition, which equates to the Old Testament of the Bible, but with Jesus recognised and accepted as the Christ (or Messiah), the redeemer of humankind. An integral part of Christianity is to spread the 'good news' of the Gospels to non-believers. Attitudes towards the Jews have been historically mixed, ranging from persecution for deicide, notably in medieval times, to support for the creation of the state of Israel as a pre-determinant of the second coming of Christ. Views on Islam differ starkly too, ranging from seeing it as an abomination because of its subversion of the essential Christian message, through to a more positive though tentative engagement based on the oneness of God (Allah simply being the Arabic word for God), a shared spiritual dimension and a large overlap on the social agenda, such as the importance of the conventional family.

Islam views itself as the last and hence the greatest of the monotheistic religions, with the Koran claimed as the word of God revealed to the Prophet Muhammad through the Archangel Gabriel over a twenty-year period. The sayings (*hadith*) and traditions (*sunna*) of the prophet have supplemented the Koran as the basis on which a good life should be lived. Ensuring that the call to Islam (*da'wa*) is heard is an integral part of the faith. Jesus is revered, but not as the Son of God. As a chronologically earlier prophet, Jesus is viewed as a subordinate figure to Muhammad. Historically, religious minorities (*dhimmi*), notably Jews and Christians, have been seen as 'people of the book' (*ahl al-kitab*), and therefore have tended not to be persecuted. The Muslim Middle East's views of the Jewish people mainly focuses on Zionism and Israel, and are more closely associated with the political situation in Palestine than the ancient world (although the Prophet Muhammad did defeat in battle a variety of Jewish tribes in Arabia, not least in Medina itself, accusing them of duplicity, a charge that is still sometimes repeated today).

Christians are viewed as fair game for conversion, a function of Islam's sense of itself as the highest of the revealed religions. There is much ignorance of Christianity in the Muslim World, with, for example, the Virgin Mary sometimes assumed to be a component of the Trinity. Attitudes ranging between puzzlement and contempt are often expressed for the way in which secularism has displaced the centrality of Christianity in Europe, in particular since the 1950s. Muslims tend, though not without exception, to view permissive social behaviour, from drug taking, through female control of sexuality, to passive participation in gay sex, with deep disapproval, and evidence that Christianity, addled by relativist values, is in rapid decline.

Political Islam

One of the most intense debates in Islam is that which relates to its political nature. In Christianity there is a long acknowledged division between the spiritual and the temporal, with the invocation to 'render unto Caesar what is Caesar's and render unto God what is God's'. This central division does not exist in anything like such an explicit form in Islam. Many Islamic theologians emphasise the comprehensive nature of the religion, and believe that it contains a prescription for all aspects of life, from the individual, familial and social to the economic and political. This helps to explain why the widespread presence of political movements based on Islamic values is not deemed to be inappropriate.

For those believing that Islam is an intrinsically political religion there is a choice of thinkers with whom to identify, covering the range from a more liberal interpretation to much more hard-line views. In brief, these can be illustrated by two Egyptian thinkers, Muhammad Abduh (1849–1905) and Sayyid Qutb (1906–66). They were products of their time: Abduh active in the late nineteenth century, when religious ideas were again in ferment; Qutb, an ideologist for the Muslim Brotherhood, spent much of his later life in jail before being executed, a victim of the illiberal struggle with the Arab nationalists. Abduh was a 'rationalist', who emphasised a freer, more discursive and interpretive approach to Islam and politics. Sayyid Qutb, increasingly embittered by his incarceration, is associated with a more uncompromising line, which preached violent *jihad*.

Another key movement within the domain of political Islam, or Islamism as it is often referred, is that of salafism, an approach identified closely with the views of Rashid Rida (1865–1935). Salafism refers to the 'pious elders', who were the first generation of the prophet's adherents. The society over which they presided is regarded as especially holy because of the direct inspiration that it drew from the founder. Only by replicating such a period can a just society have any chance of being recreated, so salafists believe.

Though salafism is by its nature a conservative ideology, one must be careful not to make the mistake that all conservatism comes from Islam or even that Islam is an essentially conservative religion. Islam is not the only important belief system in the

Middle East. Other value systems, such as tribalism (with its preoccupation with real or imagined kin relations) and patriarchy (with hierarchical, male dominated power structures based on seniority) have been important in moulding deeply embedded beliefs and attitudes. Indeed, society in the region, especially for the social and cultural elites, has not always been dominated by conservative social structures.

Standing in contrast to the notion of Islam as an intrinsically political religion are the values of secularism, which in the region are closely associated with the political values of the state in Turkey. The republican regime in Turkey was founded in the 1920s on a secular, positivist outlook that regarded Islam as the equivalent of cognitive underdevelopment. A basket of reforms was adopted to bolster secularism, including the abandonment of the Arabic script, the form in which the Koran was recorded, in favour of its Latin equivalent, and the replacement of traditional with Western-style dress. In fact the ideology adopted in Turkey was more akin to the French Third Republic concept of laicism, with its notion of the state control of religion (rather than, as a more American conception would have it, the mere separation of the two).

While Turkey was a special case, the cosmopolitan values of secularism and a polyglot cultural refinement characterised much of the educated elite in Egypt during the inter-war years. It was the influx of the conservative and superstitious countryside into the small cities of the region from the 1950s onwards, together with the narrow-minded practice of Arab nationalism, with its homogenising Sunni dominance and its persecution of ethnic minorities, which squeezed much of the life out of the pluralism of the day.

The first and most effective attempt to harness this rural to urban migration came in Egypt, with the establishment of the Muslim Brotherhood (*ikhwan al-muslimin*) in 1928. Under its dynamic young leader, Hasan al-Banna, the *ikhwan* was set up as a welfare organisation aiming to assist the new arrivals, most of whose number were poor, male and ill-equipped to make the transition to urban life. As the brotherhood gained rapid success as a social movement, it morphed into an organisation with an increasingly political outlook and message. Within two decades, the Muslim Brotherhood had become a threat to the political order. It resorted to street violence as a way of advancing its own standing. Banna himself was killed at the age of forty-two in 1949, probably at the hands of the security services. When the Free Officers coup came in 1952 the *ikhwan* was the only movement that posed a threat to Egypt's new military rulers. Five and a half decades later that same basic observation continues to describe Egyptian politics.

The brotherhood may not have been victorious politically in Egypt but the organisation would not necessarily see that as a failure. Two views of the political sphere have tended to compete within it. The dominant one, associated with the increasingly ageing leadership that grew up with Banna, sees its crucial role as building a mass Islamic community from below. To this end, the brotherhood has established an elaborate system of charitable and relief activity, aimed at attracting the urban poor to its ranks. Its greatest success was just after the Cairo earthquake of 1992, which killed 500 people, when the speed and effectiveness of the *ikhwan*'s humanitarian relief response clearly outstripped that of the state. As long as the organisation is allowed to proselytise it is willing to coexist with the ruling regime and not seek to challenge it, even putting up with periodic bouts of limited repression. By contrast, a younger, more impatient minority of the movement has been frustrated at such passivity and the long-term nature of the organisation's strategy. Elements of it have at various times since the 1970s left to form more radical splinter groups, such as the *Gama'at Islamiyya*. Though these have often resorted to violence they too have failed to deliver a radical political breakthrough.

Though the protracted stand-off between regime and opposition continues in Egypt, the Muslim Brotherhood has been rather more successful in its creation of spin-offs, now found across much of the Arab part of the region. These franchises began to emerge in the 1940s, with the creation of a Muslim Brotherhood in Jordan. Notable chapters exist in Syria, Algeria, Iraq and Palestine. These organisations are now only loosely associated with the parent movement. These franchises were created with the cooperation of the parent, working in conjunction with other nationals, some of whose leading lights would have studied in Egypt. The informal networks of scholars and activists linking the main organisation with its various spin-offs remains strong. The size, track record and length of existence of the original body in Cairo has given it a moral influence with the new groups. In spite of these considerable ties, it would be wrong to see the newer creations as an organic part of the founder body, let alone subject to its will. Hence, the Muslim Brotherhood cannot be said to form an Islamist 'International', reminiscent of the Communist International (or Comintern) of the Cold War era. The brotherhood organisation in Kuwait rapidly distanced itself from the main Muslim Brotherhood in Cairo after the Iraqi invasion of the emirate in 1990. It did so once it had become clear that the latter was unwilling to support it in its hour of need.

Islam and revolution

The fortunes of the Muslim Brotherhood demonstrate that Islam as a contemporary political force stretches back at least to the 1920s. It also shows that Islamism was an ideological movement that existed in parallel with Arab nationalism, and was not its chronological successor. Nevertheless, the fortunes of political Islam were generally subordinate to those of nationalism, certainly until the battlefield defeat of Arab nationalism's primary state sponsors in Cairo and Damascus in 1967. But it was the Iranian revolution in 1979, and the subsequent establishment of an Islamic revolutionary state, that would transform the fortunes of political Islam. Since the 1970s the greatest challenges to the established order in the Middle East have come from the forces of religious radicalism.

The origins of the Iranian revolution can be divided into long-term simmering causes and shorter run triggers. Key among the former was the way in which the second Pahlavi state was consolidated, with the young Muhammad Reza Shah returning in 1953 from a hurried flight into exile under the protection of a UK- and US-sponsored counter-revolution. The Shah's regime was then beholden to the US, as a national security structure was built up capable of facing down internal threats. The notorious SAVAK secret police was its centrepiece. As the Shah's grip on power increased he attempted to forge a platform of legitimacy, through the launching in 1963 of an ambitious strategy of economic and social change, known by the name of the 'White Revolution'. In a dry run for the later overthrow of the regime, the Shah's reforms were vigorously opposed by: the merchants of the bazaar, reacting against the newly established agri-industries that threatened their trade in such goods imported from outside; conservative social forces, reacting against attempts to modernise and mobilise female labour; and parts of the Shia ulema, who objected to the Shah's perceived secularism. With a rising clerical figure, Ruhollah Khomeini, emerging as the Shah's most implacable opponent, resistance was not easily faced down. While the Shah had no real social or economic base of support in the country, his opponents had a history of mutual collaboration.

It would be 1977 before the first real signs of revolutionary ferment would reappear in Iran. The origins of these were threefold. First, the overheating of the economy following the windfall oil rents of the previous four years. Though the economy had grown rapidly hitherto, its subsequent chronic stop-go nature would trigger a sudden burst of unemployment among recent arrivals in the cities, while a surge in inflation would accentuate urban impoverishment. Second, the election of Jimmy Carter as US president in 1977, and his introduction of a human rights conditionality into relations with even close friends like the Shah's Iran created confusion in Tehran. The perennially hypersensitive Iranians assumed that Washington had abandoned the Shah politically, in spite of many subsequent American protestations to the contrary. Third, a cycle of challenge and response emerged, involving an increasingly emboldened and broadly based opposition, versus a regime isolated and out of touch.

The year 1978 proved to be crucial. Clashes between demonstrators and the security forces became increasingly violent and frequent, as the end of traditional Shia forty-day mourning periods sparked further clashes. The oil workers strike of the autumn exposed the brittleness of the regime, which was even incapable of keeping the source of its wealth from flowing. Alternating strategies of repression and concession simply confused and demoralised the Shah's remaining supporters, while failing to elicit a positive response from leftists, liberals and Islamists across society. Attempts to emasculate a resurgent Khomeini living in exile in Iraq by pressuring his hosts to expel him backfired, as did a crude attempt at defamation, as he became more dangerous in his new, effectively unregulated exile in Paris. Finally, the early onset of the cancer that would kill him helped to debilitate the Shah, and partly disabled a system that was based around the indispensability of this one man.

With the Shah's flight in January 1979 the Iranian monarchy was finished. As in Russia in 1917, the transitional period of liberal nationalism lasted just a few months before Khomeini and his supporters mounted their own takeover. By 1981 there was no effective opposition to Khomeini and the new order of Islamic authoritarianism that it represented. What followed, until Khomeini's death in June 1989, was a regime more intent on consolidating itself than on unleashing revolutionary activism. True, there were some signs of radical change: the 444-day US embassy hostage crisis; Iran's determination to 'punish the aggressor', Saddam Hussein, during the Iran–Iraq war; the early patronage of the PLO, which was pointedly housed in the former Israeli embassy; Khomeini's formula for governance, rule by the Islamic jurist (*velayat-e faqih*), which maximised his own arbitrary authority within the system; Khomeini's opportunistic death sentence against the novelist Salman Rushdie for blasphemy, which animated much of the Muslim masses; florid rhetoric in favour of the downtrodden of the world. In reality, even these more extreme examples were either devices for the consolidation of political power or largely empty political gestures.

Once Khomeini was gone in June 1989, politics evolved inexorably in the direction of a regime based on vested interests acting for itself; Iran's own, updated version of *Animal Farm*. Policies and structures were casually abandoned, such as the move from state-centred to liberal economics, and the replacement of a parliamentary system of government by that of an executive presidency. Ali Khamenei was chosen to take over Khomeini's functions as 'leader of the revolution', even though he had indifferent political and religious credentials. Parallel military organisations, like the Revolutionary Guards (*pasdaran*), were the guarantors that there would be no counter-revolution. Posts were shuffled around the top figures within the regime, stifling pluralism. Arguably, the one exception to the rule was the election of Muhammad Khatami as president in 1997 and 2001. With seventy per cent of the popular vote on a high turnout, the candidacy of this bookish man represented the hopes of the political outside. But his gently reforming instincts proved no match for the revolutionary hardliners, who eventually stymied the country's spirit of change. Well before Khatami's election, the Iranian republic had become a device for the retention and wielding of political power, with Islam reduced to little more than a crude legitimiser.

Today, Iran no longer stands as a model for emulation across the region. It functions as a sponsor and funder of radical Islamist movements, notably Hizbollah and Hamas, which would seek to challenge the established order in Lebanon and Palestine respectively.

Islamism and opposition

Initially, there was considerable excitement in the region over the revolution in Iran. After-all, 'people power' had succeeded in getting rid of an authoritarian regime with an acknowledged tyrant at its head. The widespread existence of repressive regimes across the region meant that it was easy in theory to transpose the Iranian case to most other countries. And there were some domestic stirrings that could be linked in part at least to the general encouragement generated by the Iranian model. Most notably these included the takeover in 1979 of the Grand Mosque in Mecca by a group of several hundred Sunni radicals, led by Juhaiman al-Utaibi, opposed to the venality of the Saudi regime, and in 1981 the assassination of the Egyptian leader, Anwar Sadat, by Islamist extremists, in protest at his clampdown against political freedoms at home.

On the whole, the Iranian revolution has proved to be more of a strange anachronism than a viable example of regional change. This was partly because of the unusual nature of the case: overwhelmingly Shiite; ethnically fifty per cent Persian and with only a small Arab minority; and the state-dependent nature of organised religion in the Sunni countries, in contrast to the financial and intellectual independence of Shiism. It was also in part because less than two years after the ousting of the Shah the Islamic regime helped precipitate the Iran–Iraq war. By 1982, the war had developed into what Arabs increasingly perceived to be a war of Persian expansionism, no different from those that had punctuated the uneasy relationship between the Arab and Persian ethnicities over the preceding millennium and a half.

The Iranian revolution may have quickly evolved into a regional anachronism, but it did not mean that political Islam as a focus of anti-regime activism was of marginal importance. The defeat and disillusionment widely felt towards Arab nationalism after 1967 left an ideological void at the centre of the ideas debate in the region. Other competing ideological movements seemed ill-placed to fill the gap: socialism had been discredited by the crude expansion of the Arab state in the 1950s and 1960s; Communism historically made little impact beyond Iran, Iraq and Syria, its godlessness placing it at a disadvantage in its search for mass activism; liberalism was too closely associated with the status quo politics of the US. Islamism was a political movement of potential that seemed to have few viable rivals.

Those with an anti-regime bias would embrace Islamism in its various forms across the region from the 1970s onwards. They did so, first, because of the accessibility of the idiom that it used. Islamic ideas in political form seemed to diagnose the Arab predicament and present culturally appropriate blueprints for change. Incumbent regimes were viewed at best as self-serving cliques; at worst as godless abominations. In Saudi Arabia, one of the US's closest allies in the region, the Al Saud leadership was damned for peddling what was labelled as 'American Islam'. Across the region Islamist groupings increasingly proclaimed the slogan that 'Islam is the solution' (*Islam huwa al-hal*).

They did so, second, because of the practical opportunities that organised religion might afford. In highly repressive contexts, only the mosque and the religious school (*madrassa*) offered a legitimate focus where activists might come together, build up networks and exchange literature and ideas. The case of Algeria is especially instructive. Only through religious institutions could the one party state of the Front Liberation National (FLN), with repressive military power behind it, be effectively challenged. The outcome was the emergence of the broad-based and religiously inclined Front Islamique du Salut (FIS), which fleetingly seemed poised to inherit political power when the authoritarian regime crumbled in 1988.

From the 1970s through the 1990s it seemed as if politics in the Middle East had become polarised between two extremes. On the one side there was the extreme of state power, wielded by an ageing leadership determined to hang on to office for as long as possible, and greatly reliant on the heavy hand of repression. On the other, there was the main opposition movement, increasingly Islamist in complexion, and willing over time owing to a convergence of interest to absorb something of a liberal agenda in arguing for globalised standards of human rights and political pluralism. In reality, the former found it relatively easy to intimidate Western governments into believing that they were the only bulwark against the wildfire of Islamist radicalism that might spread as fast as it had been feared Communism might spread through east Asia in the 1960s. The nature of the role of political opposition, with its negative assaults on government policies, and the vague articulation of a political utopia, seemed to confirm the fears of that which was posed by the Islamist opposition. Hence, the limited and low key protestations when the army moved in to subvert an election process that was set to deliver a sweeping FIS win at the polls in Algeria in early 1992.

In spite of this dominant story of competition and confrontation between political regime and oppositionist Islamism, this is not the only experience in the region. There have been situations where regimes and Islamists have coexisted successfully enough. Interestingly, this has tended to take place where there is no ingrained experience of violent confrontation, and where something of an institutional political framework already exists to contain and channel the rivalry. The longest running example of political accommodation exists in Jordan, where the Muslim Brotherhood supported the Hashemite regime in facing down the challenges from radical nationalism in the 1950s. By the 1970s the brotherhood had moved into opposition, a position in which it has become entrenched since 1989 with the return to an invigorated but restricted parliamentary life in the kingdom. Hitherto, the *ikhwan* has functioned as a loyal opposition, at least among East Bank Jordanians (as opposed to the more radical Palestinian membership) in the movement.

Kuwait is another example where Islamism has been woven into the fabric of representative life. Indeed, in the emirate there are routinely at least three de facto Islamist parties represented in the National Assembly, a Shia Islamist association and two Sunnis, one with its origins in the Muslim Brotherhood. One may argue that since the 1990s some of the more mainstream Islamist parties have begun the process of socialisation into a more pluralist, representational politics through the limited democratisation from above that has come partially to characterise political life during that time.

For the best hope that there can be a historic reconciliation between democratic politics and Islamist political movements one has to go to Turkey, a country that has enjoyed aspects of democratic practice since 1946. The election of the Islamist Justice and Development Party (AKP) in 2002 and the years that it has subsequently spent as the governing party has taught it that it has an interest in the maintenance of the democratic process. With the AKP (and its predecessor parties) having dominated municipal politics since 1994, there is as yet no record of the party relinquishing power as a result of the electoral expression of the general will. The political standoff between the AKP and the Constitutional Court in 2008 suggests that it is the AKP's hard-line secular opponents who now fear that they have nothing to gain from participation in an electoral democracy. With institutional politics in Turkey suddenly more fragile than it has seemed since the early 1990s, the chances of blending oppositionist Islamism and hard regime power in a virtuous mix of stable, good governance, though still likely is certainly not inevitable.

Islam and terrorism

All of the nineteen hijackers involved in the 9/11 attacks were from the Middle East. Their leader, Muhammad Atta, was an Egyptian; the largest country contingent came from Saudi Arabia, with fifteen of the nineteen participants (two others were from the UAE and one from Lebanon). In spite of the infamous nature of the attacks they were just the latest example of a close link between terrorism and the Middle East. This link goes back to the 1950s and the use of violence against non-combatants by fringe Palestinian liberation groups. It encompasses infamous outrages like the attack by a Palestinian group on the Israeli team at the Munich Olympics in 1972. More recently, it has become associated with other countries in the region, notably Turkey in the 1970s, Lebanon in the late 1970s and 1980s, and Iraq in the 2000s, amply illustrating that the peoples of the region have become the biggest victims of regional terrorism. Arguably the Iraqi case is the most acute of all of the above because of the industrial nature of the scale of human destruction perpetrated by al-Qaida and its affiliates in Iraq between 2004 and 2007.

It should not need to be stated that while terrorism and the Middle East and more latterly terrorism and Islam are often bracketed together the relationship is not an exclusive one. The

DEFINING TERRORISM

In spite of many attempts, there has been no internationally recognised definition of terrorism. It is often said that one man's freedom fighter is another man's terrorist. It is, however, possible to define terrorism in terms of the nature of the act. 'The deliberate use or credible threat of the use of violence against civilians with the intention of achieving mass intimidation in order to bring about political goals.' In the aftermath of 9/11, a clear act of terror, the EU stated forthrightly that it opposed the pursuit of political aims employing the means of terrorism, even when the objectives were accepted as wholly legitimate, as in the case of the Palestinian people's desire to end occupation.

notion of 'terror' first arose with the French Revolution and the 'reign of terror'. In its form as an instrument of violent opposition politics, terrorist violence stretches back at least some 120 years to the social revolutionaries in the political ferment of late nineteenth-century Russia, and the anarchist movement in Europe in the early twentieth century. Since then many liberation groups have used terror as a political instrument, from the radical Zionists of the 1940s to Irish republicans, the fringe of the extreme left in Germany and Italy, to the Tamil 'Tigers' in Sri Lanka and various Kashmiri groups. Indeed, there have been occasions when some commentators have casually and erroneously attributed terrorist attacks to a Middle East connection, the 1995 Oklahoma bombing being a good example. In general, though terrorism is not by any means an exclusively Middle Eastern or Islamic phenomenon, there have been those in the region prepared to use such justification for their acts of violence.

The Middle East has been the birthplace of the world's three leading monotheistic religions. As a reflection of this, it is awash with religious-cum-historical monuments that rival any of the great architectural tributes to the greatness of God in Europe. There has been no mass movement for secularism in the region. Only in Turkey has secularism become entrenched, and even there it is very much associated with the ruling elite. That leaves religion as a ubiquitous presence. It features prominently as part of the identity of Muslims, Christians and Jews across the region. It is a rich source of cultural expression, political values and philosophical debate.

The self-consciously political expression of Islam has been part of the market place of ideas in the region since at least the 1920s. Since the defeat of Egypt and the discrediting of its Arab nationalist creed in the 1967 war, political Islam has been the ideology most capable of mobilising the people of the region. The Iranian revolution of 1979 showed the potential of people-power allied with a strong political message. Since then, most of the regimes of the region have come under pressure to some degree from Islamism. In spite of the promise of radical change, political Islam has remained an opposition ideology, unable to force widespread regime change. Only in the periphery of the region – Iran and Sudan – has change actually taken place in its name. The region appears frozen in a polarised struggle between regime authoritarians and opposition Islamism. Frustrated by such a stalemate, many radical Islamist activists have drifted into the twilight orbit of militant transnationalism, most notoriously epitomised by the activities of al-Qaida and its affiliates. An interesting experiment with political Islam in a democratic setting has taken place in Turkey since 2002. For mainstream Islamism in the Arab world, the Turkish example shows how democratic practice can be used to gain and retain power indefinitely in the future, should they be given the initial chance.

10

Gender

In 2002 a groundbreaking UN report identified the absence of female mobilisation as one of the three main elements retarding the development of the Arab world. (The others were negligible political freedoms and the absence of a knowledge economy.) Although written by Arab intellectuals and published in Arabic, the impact of the report has been limited. As before, the political and social constraints on shifts in gender power are profound. Though women's participation in Arab society is growing at the margins, Arab society, and the Middle East more generally, remains overwhelmingly and suffocatingly patriarchal.

Out of sight, out of mind

In the early 1980s, having returned to Britain following a four-year stint in Riyadh, the former British ambassador to Saudi Arabia was asked a question about what women in the kingdom think. 'I don't know,' replied the envoy with disarming honesty. 'I didn't meet any.' The response did not suggest indolence or a dereliction of duty. Rather, it reflected Saudi social mores and conventions. All of the senior Saudi political hierarchy were men. Contact between Saudi women and men who are non-family members is discouraged. In public, all women are required to wrap themselves in an all-enveloping black garment (*abaya*), such modesty codes being enforced by a dedicated and at times over-zealous religious police (*mutawa*), who use canes to inflict pain and humiliation on those whom they consider to be non-compliant. On one infamous occasion a member of the religious police unwittingly set about the American ambassador's wife for an indiscretion of dress.

Women's ability to travel is circumscribed because of the ban on driving, and the proscription on travelling abroad without specific permission being given by a father, brother or husband. Invitations to dinner would have involved strict gender segregation, with the wives of foreign diplomats being whisked away into the secluded family space of the household, only to reappear at the end of the evening having been fed and watered separately.

Although arguably the most extreme case of gender segregation in the Middle East, Saudi Arabia is far from being unrepresentative. Women are subject to strict codes of dress when out in public in Iran; anecdotes about acid being thrown in the faces of the 'immodest', though dating largely from the early years of the revolution, are still often repeated. Classes at the national university in Qatar are separated on the basis of sex. Social relations are as conservative and dependent in the Kurdish backwater of south-east Turkey as anywhere else in the region. Segregated dinner parties in the home are the norm in Jordan, among indigenous Christian families as well as Muslims.

How does one explain such extremes of social conservatism? One needs to look for a combination of material and cultural explanations. In the case of the former, the impetus was shaped by the realities of economic and physical security in a marginal ecology, lacking rule of law. In the semi-nomadic, livestock herding context of the tribe, where grazing pasture and wells were vital to survival, the functional division of labour of the unit reflected those of physical gender characteristics in a pre-contraception age. Women, with their multiple pregnancies, spent much of their adult lives carrying, suckling or nurturing the young. Only men were available to develop their prowess on horse or camel-back and to fight to preserve the source of the tribe's prosperity. Stories of manly heroics were then spun and embellished in an oral culture, which prized recitation around the campfire, a medieval scene evocative of the satirical writings of Chaucer in *The Knight's Tale*.

As such relationships became entrenched by the necessities of material well-being, a value system began to emerge that sought to justify such practices on moral grounds. This was the code of tribal honour, which was purported to rest with the young females of the tribe. As long as chaste before marriage, dressed conservatively from the onset of puberty and demur in their conduct, the tribe could be proud of its young girls. Invocations especially on female modesty were mined and expropriated from Islamic scripture to underpin the message. For women and girls, departing from these expectations was a risky business because of the effect that it could have on the reputation of men. Refusal to accept actual or symbolic seclusion risked provoking the chaos or irrational activity (*fitna*), which often afflicts human beings in their romantic behaviour. To ward off the enormity of such threats serious measures were believed to be required, and could result in incarceration, physical abuse, or, in the extreme, death if the collective reputation of the tribe was placed in jeopardy. Over time such beliefs became more cynically instrumentalised. In Turkey 'a hand above her head [implying chastisement] and a baby in her stomach' is a well-known aphorism of how a man should best go about taming and controlling his wife.

'HONOUR' KILLINGS

Honour killings are a feature of traditional society across much of the Muslim World, including Afghanistan and Pakistan as well as many of the countries of the Middle East such as Egypt, Jordan, Syria and others. They are not limited to Arab society, some of the worst excesses of such practices occurring among Kurdish

'HONOUR' KILLINGS (*cont.*)

communities in south-east Turkey. The Turkish Kurdish diaspora in countries such as Germany and Sweden, where girls can easily end up being torn by the conflicting values of traditional and modern society, is identified with some of the more sickening examples of the practice. The logic goes as follows: where a female is perceived to have soiled the family honour only her death at the hands of a near relative may redeem it. In the Middle East itself, it is difficult to estimate the incidence level of honour crimes. Many go unreported or are dealt with quietly at a local level. Where the formal legal machinery comes into play there is often a dual track treatment of honour and other crimes, with the perpetrators of the former receiving lesser sentences. As with female circumcision (a practice directed at the same ends, but in which women are usually more directly complicit), since the 1980s honour killing has emerged as a fiercely contested practice, with campaigns both inside and outside the region aimed at curtailing it. In some traditional societies such campaigns have elicited a backlash, with local leaders objecting to Western interference in what are claimed to be culturally indigenous practices.

Women in politics

In 1934, just six years after the introduction of universal suffrage in Britain, women received the right to vote in parliamentary elections in independent Turkey. Though still an authoritarian state with one party rule, the move was made more as a badge of modernity than of democracy. With women an active part of the erudite strata in leading urban centres like Beirut and Cairo, it seemed plausible that the profile of women in society would rise with the emergence of an independent set of aspiring new states.

As we now know that pathway was not taken. In the 1950s the old social classes were swept away by the new, lower middle class revolutionaries, with their more introspective conception of appropriate behaviour. The emergence of the male-only military as the main vehicle for political challenge and consolidation by definition excluded women from playing even a supporting role in the political process. The growing conservatism of society, first under the Orwellian radicals, and then under the more restrictive atmosphere generated by religious conservatives from the 1970s onwards made it harder for secular women to pursue a role in public life. Even in the so-called vanguard of women's rights, Turkey, the proportion of women MPs in 1935 was at 4.6% more than it was in 1999 (4%).

In purely statistical terms women have been more visible in the political life of the region since the late 1980s, but incrementally and patchily so, and very much from a low base. Take for example the executive level of cabinet government. Tokenism abounds. Kuwait and Qatar only saw their first female ministers appointed in the 2000s.

Even where a tradition of senior women political figures is beginning to build up there are still constraints. Jordan has had female ministers since the early 1980s. Initially, such service took place in 'soft' ministries, such as social development, which are perceived as naturally the home of the feminine. These Cinderella ministries tend to be low on budgets and the capacity to act, and are taken about as seriously as the portfolios of culture and of sport. Since those early days, women have worked their way up the hierarchy of cabinet posts, a handful of Jordanian women occupying such positions as ministers of information, planning, industry and even (one of three) deputy premiers. Tellingly, however, the critical posts of defence, finance, the interior and of course the premiership itself, the macho ministries, have eluded them. Recently, Jordan introduced a small number of parliamentary seats reserved exclusively for women, in despair at their inability to win places through conventional means. This has placed Jordanian women, more than fifty per cent of the population, in the same category as the county's tiny religious and ethnic minorities in having reserved representation. It goes without saying that dynastic succession moves strictly through male lines.

The record of limited visibility is comparable to the conservative monarchies even in places where one might expect a record of greater female participation. In sophisticated Lebanon women cannot make a serious impression on the executive because of the prevalence of old militia leaders, who, since the end of the civil war in 1990, have crowded out the senior posts of state. In Palestine there have only been two women ministers of any profile since the Palestinian Authority was set up in 1995, both of them in their own ways unrepresentative of their sex. Um Jihad was appointed to the cabinet by President Arafat because she was the widow of Abu Jihad (Khalil al-Wazir), the PLO leader assassinated by Israel in Tunis before the onset of the Oslo peace-making process in the 1990s. Her elevation was more a posthumous tribute to a fellow Arafat stalwart than a recognition of her own capabilities. Arguably the best-known Palestinian woman is also the least representative. Hanan Ashrawi is a Protestant Christian, who was educated at a Quaker School in the West Bank, her individuality of background making her of no threat to the social stability of the family hierarchy under conservative Christians, let alone Muslims. In Iraq, also with a reputation for being 'progressive', twenty-five per cent representation in the National Assembly is reserved for women. This was a stipulation of the new political system demanded by its American occupiers (though not itself implemented by them at home).

It is, of course, important to place the low visibility of women in public life in proper perspective. It was only in 1979 that Britain elected its first female prime minister. The number of women in legislatures across the Western world is still well below their profile within society. This reality may also be seen in Israel, the society that most closely resembles a Western society in the Middle East. Israel has only had one female premier, Golda Meir, in the early 1970s. Until the 1990s Israeli cabinets only included the odd woman. In 2008 Israel had a female foreign minister, Tzipi Livni, and there were two other women ministers out of a cabinet of twenty-six, but that comprises less than ten per cent of the positions. The role of women in the labour force, however, comfortably outstrips its Middle Eastern rivals. The glass ceiling facing female promotion within the military, a persistent barrier to women's wider political ambitions, is in the process of being dismantled.

It would not be entirely right to give the impression that there are no politically influential women in the Middle East. But they tend to be urban rather than rural, educated rather than uneducated, high born rather than modest of background. The most potentially influential of all women in the region are undoubtedly those who are close to the top echelons of the regimes, especially the leader himself. The most recent version of this phenomenon is that of the 'First Ladies', where the wives of the region's leaders have come together to promote favoured political or social goals. The Arab First Ladies have emerged as a not inconsiderable force for the promotion of women's interests, especially in the field of education. They provide a forum within which the wives of conservative Gulf leaders, traditionally silent and kept out of sight, can emerge as national figures. A First Ladies group was created as a vehicle for the collection of humanitarian aid for the Palestinians of Gaza in 2009 in the midst of the Israeli military onslaught. Created by Emine Erdogan, the wife of the Turkish prime minister, it provided an additional and crucially female dimension through which political leaders could associate themselves with popular causes.

At an individual country level, Asma al-Asad, is an active and intelligent consort to the Syrian leader, Bashar al-Asad. His sister, Bushra al-Asad, the wife of the chief of military intelligence, Asif Shawkat, has been described as the brightest of the Asad clan and may be presumed to have influence as a function of access, even if her sex debars her from wielding power directly. The women of the ruling Sabah family have their own political salon *(diwan)*, and some of them joined the wider demand for female enfranchisement in Kuwait in the 1990s. Suzanne Mubarak of Egypt, and Jordan's two most recent queens, the feisty Arab-American, Noor, and the incumbent Palestinian–Jordanian, Rania, have been elegant and effective advocates for their husbands around the world. Suha Arafat tried to play such a role and fell embarrassingly short, lacking both character and discretion. In Qatar, the Emir's second wife, Shaikha Mozah Bint Nasser al-Missned, has been the driving force behind educational reform in the emirate. While such women have sought to maximise their impact on politics like the wives and mothers of sultans for hundreds of years, the fact remains that their role is largely confined to that of 'pillow influence'. As the countless wives (though never more than four at a time for reasons of religious sensitivities) of the likes of King Abdul Aziz of Saudi Arabia and Emir Jaber of Kuwait, attest, they always remain vulnerable to dismissal.

Fighting over women

The absence of women from positions of real power in the Middle East does not mean that they are a marginal or forgotten group. Perish the thought that they should be so lucky. Since the onset of colonialism women have been important as a contested group in Middle Eastern societies, but largely as objects, rather than as active and sentient players. Repeatedly, those espousing the values of modernity and change have argued that women should be taken out of seclusion, should have their various head covers removed and should be mobilised as part of the labour force. This was the case during Lord Cromer's Egypt across the turn of the nineteenth and twentieth centuries. This was a central aspect of the core vision of Ataturk in Turkey in the 1920s and 1930s. It was shared by his reforming admirer and contemporary, Reza Shah Pahlavi, in Iran, and repeated by his son, Muhammed Reza Pahlavi in the early 1960s.

In all such cases, women were a major arena in which such social and political trials of power were played out. The early anti-colonialists in places like Algeria held onto the veil, no longer as a symbol of social conservatism but ironically as a modern badge of anti-imperial resistance. In the highly conservative, rurally dominated areas of Turkey and Iran regime opponents could rally support on the back of the woman question more easily than any other issue. It could be argued that the second Pahlavi Shah never really recovered from his vilification as a cipher for the sort of 'Westoxification' that the rights of women, mocked as 'the Shah's painted dolls', were widely associated with. The issue of how women should dress, how and when they should engage with public life and what roles might be considered appropriate for them had become easily conflated with the leading political issues of the day.

If women have been used by self-proclaimed modernisers to drag societies into a setting of social and economic advancement, so have they been used by conservative forces to resist the encroachment of contemporary, globalising phenomena, from American military power to Western consumer culture to ideas of female emancipation. In the Arab world, women wearing headscarves in cities have gone from the rare and exceptional in the early 1970s to the ubiquitous and dominant three decades later. In post-US invasion Iraq, society has turned to its religious leaders for comfort and security. That can be measured in part by the modest dress sense of women visible on the street. In Cairo too, formerly the bastion of Arab secularism, the headscarf and other signs of piety are difficult to avoid, a response in part perhaps to the controversial peace with Israel, and the economic dependency of post-1980 Egypt on the US.

INTERNATIONAL CONFERENCE ON POPULATION & DEVELOPMENT, CAIRO 1994

In 1994 the latest in a series of themed world conferences on the issue of world population was held in Cairo. Officials, advocates, and experts from across the planet arrived in the Egyptian capital for a week's worth of deliberations. The agenda of the conference was an essentially liberal one, spanning such issues as birth control, abortion, women's rights, teenage pregnancy and female reproductive health. There had been some controversy before the arrival of the participants, mainly between the Vatican and the radical feminist agenda over the issue of abortion. By the start of proceedings the moral pressure of the Vatican seemed to have been successfully resisted. Regarded as a diplomatic success for Egypt, the conference began with the national media reporting the various events approvingly and in detail. After a couple of days, however, non-elite Egyptians began to focus on the nature of the occasion that their country was hosting, and found its substance far from entirely to their liking. The Islamist opposition quickly took up the issue and preached against the inferred permissiveness of the occasion. Opposition to the meeting snowballed. Suddenly, the authorities in Cairo found themselves on the defensive. Media coverage was significantly reduced. It was with almost visible relief that the Egyptian government packed off the participants, once the formal sessions were over.

That leaves tiny islands of egalitarian change in the region. Tunisia, with a population of twelve million, some three per cent of the Arab total, is clearly the most liberal of the Arab countries as far as women are concered, its egalitarian policies adopted by the founder of the modern state, Habib Bourgeiba. The 1956 Code of Personal Status established the principle of equality of rights before the law, and, among other things, outlawed polygamy and extended equal rights to divorce. Abortion in early stage pregnancy is available. State grants exist for business start-ups. A quarter of judges and one-third of lawyers are women. Elite women are the primary beneficiaries of this more open social system. For most of their sex, however, even in Tunisia, these rights remain notional and law courts a distant arbiter. And it remains very difficult for a Tunisian woman of any background to live alone.

Other changes burnish less brightly. The 2003 penal code reforms have placed Morocco second in the provision of formal rights for women in the Arab world, making it a sort of 'Tunisia lite'. The new package was handed down in a speech from the throne, emphasising the direction in which reforms flow in the region. Kuwait introduced female suffrage on the same basis as for men in 2005. The representational reforms from above in Qatar have been introduced on the basis of women having the vote. The experiences of Egypt are that 'progressive' change can be thrown into reverse as well as driven forward. Family status provisions adopted in 1979 were rolled back in 1985.

Generally, though, the position of women has been coming under increasing pressure in three ways. First, because regimes seeking to fend off conservative political pressure from the Islamist right tend to look at women's issues (as opposed to high political issues, such as foreign and defence policy) as areas where policy concessions can be made relatively cost free. Second, there is the difficulty of implementing existing legal statutes that favour women. This is owing to the slowness and inefficiencies of judicial systems across the region, notably in the areas of family law, divorce and inheritance. Women for instance can come under intense pressure from male members of their family to forego their inheritance rights regardless of the formal provisions in place. Third, through persisting levels of illiteracy, especially in rural areas, which in turn make it difficult for women to discover and demand their rights.

It is now a conventional wisdom of development studies that an empowered woman provides the best chance for a low income family to navigate away from poverty and its associated conditions, such as poor health and low educational achievement, and attain levels of increased prosperity. That is a principle that most Middle Eastern societies have yet to appreciate and internalise.

The feminist responses

In the early days of feminism, small numbers of young women in the more cosmopolitan centres of the region, such as Beirut, Cairo and Tehran, were tempted to adopt the latest fashions of their equivalents in the West. Their action was more akin to an imitation of Western practices than to an embrace of the values behind them. Such acts were largely devoid of a conscious political message. Such garments tended to clash with the traditional sartorial conservatism of the region, with the emphasis that it placed on women covering their legs, arms and shoulders, and men keeping their shirts on and eschewing the wearing of shorts. Where there were demands from a small number of isolated regional feminists for gender equality, justified on the grounds of principle alone, this was easily faced down by voices representing the forces of propriety.

The second wave of feminism has been less naive and rather more thoughtful in its strategy than its forebears. It has sought to justify gender equality by marshalling evidence from indigenous experience. It has tried to sidestep the accusation that it is disloyal to its cultural roots. The debate about women has tended to revolve around the historical experience of the region. Middle Eastern feminists have pointed to the profile and importance of women's roles. Take the life of the Prophet Muhammad. He started his career as a younger husband, subsidised by his first and, until her death, sole wife, Khadija, who was herself a successful businesswoman, actively engaged in commerce. A subsequent wife of Muhammad's, Aisha, supposedly his favourite, was the daughter of Muhammad's successor, Abu Bakr and was present at the Prophet's death. The prophet's daughter, Fatima, was an important figure for Shiism, having married the man who would come to be revered as its founder, Ali ibn Abu Taleb, the 'Imam Ali,' and being the mother of Imam Hussein. She met a martyr's death along with her husband. More broadly, it has not been difficult to find countless examples of capable and ambitious women in the region, some of whom have manipulated their weaker menfolk into positions of formal importance.

The debate between second wave feminists and traditionalists has also led to arguments about how to interpret Islam's sacred texts. To take a notable example, look at the Koranic limitation on the number of wives a man might have simultaneously to four. From today's perspective this looks like an indulgence of man's carnal inclinations. Feminists have argued that by culturally and historically contextualising the statement one can see that the intention was to end the previous practice of men taking unlimited numbers of spouses, while emphasising that the practice of multiple wives is only permissible if one treats each wife equally. From this perspective such a reading of sacred texts emphasises responsible action and mutual respect.

Yet more recently, the debate about the role and expectations of women has expanded beyond a central, conservative-progressive rights cleavage to include activist women Islamists. They have argued that conservative dress helps to liberate women because it saves them from the physical objectification which bedevils women in the West. They argue that if a woman's body has been de-sexualised the success of that woman in the workplace is more likely to be a reflection of her talents and abilities. In some cases, women Islamists have even become assertive within their own movements. Female party activists in Turkey's Islamist movement of the mid-1990s, the Welfare Party, bemoaned the absence of women on the party's electoral list. They argued that the party's growing success owed much to the networks it provided for new arrivals in the cities from the countryside, these networks being provided primarily for women by women. After initial misgivings, the party leadership relented, and it has since become common practice for Turkey's Islamist parties to include a modest number of women on the party's slate.

It would be misleading to imply that Islamist women are anywhere near thrusting and ambitious enough for a role in public life. The majority accept the biological determinism prescribed by the men of religion and their activist male adherents. Under scrutiny, they protest that men and women are equal but different. They insist that no role is more beautiful or necessary than to provide the glue for a family and to nurture children. Even many intelligent and educated women in the more sophisticated societies of the region willingly accept such a life and insist that it delivers both self-fulfilment and a sense of worth.

Women and change

The ingrained nature of gender roles in the Middle East, entrenched by social structure and the instrumentalised use of religion, makes the outlook for change rather discouraging from the perspective of equality. However, the situation in the Middle East is not necessarily any more infelicitous than it was in Europe and North America in the nineteenth century. In those regions the prospect for gender equality, especially in such areas as employment and formal rights, was immeasurably accelerated by the outbreak of war. The experience of the Middle East since the 1960s suggests that the region is just as susceptible to transformation by cataclysmic contingencies, though not irreversibly so.

An early sign that women's roles might change quickly under

exceptional circumstances came during the Algerian struggle for independence. The revolutionaries discovered that women were not searched by the French authorities and therefore could more easily transport munitions and even bombs. Faced with such realities, the anti-colonial movement showed a deftness of tactical touch and enlisted women for such activities, the success of which has been acknowledged very recently by the use of female suicide bombers by Palestinian radicals and in Iraq.

Resistance and revolution has also helped mobilise women. In 1978 Iran, women participated in mass demonstrations against the Shah and joined the ranks of the various radical splinter groups seeking to end his rule. The courage shown by women in such a highly charged context was real enough, as many were killed, especially as the Shah's troops fired on the demonstrators indiscriminately. During the first Palestinian uprising (*intifada*) in 1987 and after, women played a pivotal role in the civil society movements of the day. While the world fixated on male youths pelting Israeli soldiers with rocks, it was the women of the West Bank and Gaza that kept the effort going, once the Israeli authorities had interned more than 10,000 of the Palestinians' overwhelmingly male activist leaders. Grass roots associations kept up the provision of primary health care and education during this time, in the most part due to women's organisational abilities and efforts.

In all three cases – Algeria, Iran and the Palestinian territories – the new political circumstances had given women an opportunity to show their effectiveness and to prove their commitment to the cause. In none of these cases, however, did women go on to play a significant political role in the affairs of their people, in spite of these initial opportunities. In part this was because the three cases were fundamentally concerned with struggles against colonial domination, tyranny and occupation respectively, rather than female emancipation in itself. Indeed, in many cases, women were happy to vacate the positions that they had held once their menfolk were able to resume their roles. Moreover, women were equally likely to be fragmented politically among the disparate ideological groups that comprised the Iranian revolution, or across the various Palestinian factions, than united in a perceived collection of gender interests.

One potentially less easily reversible agent for change is war, especially war that is of an extended duration, and profound in its effects, such as in the significant numbers of casualties that result. The 1980–88 Iran–Iraq War was one such event. The impact of the war on Iranian society was relatively limited, as the Iranian war effort was based on a male volunteer army, which was largely available on a seasonal basis. The impact of the war on Iraqi society was more far-reaching. At any one time around one-quarter of the Iraqi adult, male population was under arms. This left a gaping hole in the civilian economy, especially as far as the labour pool was concerned. Women made good this gap. The relatively competent education services available in Iraq to urban women meant that the potential for female mobilisation was already high. Moreover, Ba'thist ideology had set the tone, through the emphasis placed on the necessity of the mobilisation of women labour as part of its millennial goal of an Arab greatness restored.

In the end, the outcome of the Iran–Iraq War was not as encouraging as it might have been for the cause of women's rights. The end of hostilities left Iraq with a devastated economy. Social pressures for demobilisation started to push women out of the economy and back into the home. Out of expediency, Ba'thist propaganda began to emphasise the desirability of large families rather than the benefits of women in the workforce; Saddam Hussein, with his five children, unsurprisingly became its ideal. The introduction of UN sanctions against Iraq because of its 1990 invasion of Kuwait undermined much of what was left of the national economy. Displaced from the formal economy, Iraqi women had to search hard for any way to make a living. At the extreme of experience, many women turned to prostitution as a source of income, especially among the Iraqis that had fled to Jordan in search of a better life. A 'faith campaign' in the 1990s aimed at mobilising conservative religious values in the service of the regime had as a corollary the active discouragement of women as public workers. A case that might have been highly favourable for the cause of women's mobilisation had ended up less well placed than at the outset.

In the absence of revolution and war as drivers of social change it is perhaps to economics that one should look for a greater promise of transformation. Here, ironically, the most interesting developments have taken place in Saudi Arabia. The strict segregation of the sexes has resulted over time in the emergence of a parallel, gendered economy. So, for example, a parallel banking sector, with a separate space for female customers, staffed by women-only tellers, has emerged to service the female economy. These recent developments have given hope to women graduates that they might look forward to a professional career beyond graduation. At present, more than fifty per cent of graduates from Saudi universities are women, but the jobs market has been largely beyond them, at least until now.

A second way in which the economic lot of women in the kingdom has been changing relates to the deployment of private assets for business purposes. The recession of the mid to late 1990s led Saudi economic decision-makers to act innovatively to mobilise private savings in the interests of the national economy. One way in which they did so was to try to encourage female nationals to invest their savings locally, especially in business. In this they achieved some success, particularly among educated and well-connected women, who controlled significant assets, and had the social contacts to be able to establish and develop their own enterprises. These women were still hamstrung by the constraints on travel, and found it difficult to establish working connections with a male professional world of accountants and lawyers. Despite such annoying encumbrances, many of these women have persisted and have even achieved lucrative success.

The most severe of tests for these companies has come during the new era of super-rents from hydrocarbons, which has rendered women's capital less important since the early 2000s. Nevertheless, the decision of the Olayan group, one of the biggest and best-known conglomerates in the country, to appoint a women, Lubna Olayan, as CEO of the group's holding company in the kingdom, indicates both the importance of symbolic successes and that, in spite of regressive experiences in the wider region, a return to the old ways, even in such a socially conservative country as Saudi Arabia, is never entirely possible.

Maleness and gender

It is important to remember that gender is not just about women. In the Middle East men find themselves with narrow parameters as far as local cultural conceptions of masculinity is concerned. Some take to these roles with alacrity. The tradition of the street tough (*kabadayi*), who polices the neighbourhood in a rough and ready sort of way has a strong tradition going back to Ottoman times. The notion of the gang leader/power broker (*zaim*) is a familiar one in Lebanese history.

But these roles clearly do not suit all men. Breaking out of these peer and family-enforced near-caricatures is not easy and may attract ridicule or even violent responses if attempted. Simply avoiding such roles may prove to be costly. In different parts of the region, from the militias in Lebanon in the 1970s and 1980s, the Village Guards in the Kurdish parts of Turkey since the 1980s, the militias in Algeria since the onset of civil war in the early 1990s and the militias in Iraq since 2003 the easiest and most lucrative way for a young male with limited education to make a good living has been to join a private army. This has involved military training, drilling, the adoption of a code of discipline and over time a creeping brutalisation. It has re-enforced perceptions of masculinity that has left little room for the less respected, feminised values of compassion, under-standing and tenderness. The veiling and subordination of these feminised values may go some way towards explaining the acts of extreme brutality that have punctuated the experiences of the region, from the massacre of vulnerable Palestinians at the Sabra and Shatilla camps in Beirut by Phalangists in 1982 to the violent Kurdish insurgency and the hard response of the Turkish state, which have cost over 30,000 lives since 1984, to the throat slitting of the Islamist extremists and their state sponsored militia opponents in places like Algeria in the 1990s and more recently the fondness for beheadings among the bin Laden wannabees in the region.

Such militaristic values have increasingly been generalised and confused with norms of behaviour across the region. In the 1950s and 1960s it was the army officer, almost certainly a participant in revolutionary change, who was the admired figure. This sense of respect was largely given uncritically. It was too easily identified with a swaggering style, a dehumanising uniform and the vanity of power. The ineffectualness and self-serving nature of the reality of military rule across the region was for a long time ignored in its masculine preoccupation with the superficial.

From the late 1960s onwards it is the guerrilla fighters (*fedayeen*) that have provided the main image for such male hero worship. In the early part of this period it was the Palestinian 'freedom fighter' that most closely conformed to this view. From the 1990s it has been the guerrillas of Hizbollah, an altogether more ruthless and effective force, which has been the subject of regional adulation. The image of the Hizbollah fighter, with nothing but small arms, faith and manliness, facing down the might of Israel's sophisticated military and instilling fear in the once omnipotent Israelis in its acknowledged victory in the thirty-three day war of 2006 has captured the perceptions of male youth across the region. Images of rocket and gun-toting members of Hizbollah drilling in the streets of Beirut, rendered more feared and admired by the Shia cult of martyrdom, and the implied willingness to make the ultimate personal sacrifice, has increasingly come to dominate definitions of masculinity in the region.

Other conceptions of male success, which potentially might compete with the gun-toting guerrilla, are few and far between. The wealthy businessman, personified by the Dubai brand, is more the product of a state-led crony capitalism than genuine enterprise. The regional soccer star is unlikely to make it to the top of the elite leagues in Europe, though when he does, as with Zinedine Zidane, the adulation is his, even if his success has come with a French passport. The regionally acclaimed poet, like the recently departed Palestinian, Mahmoud Darwish, has to retain at very least an ambivalence towards the dominant regional values of maleness in order to retain credibility with his core readership.

With such images rampant in the region, it has not proved possible to leave such brutalisation in the public sphere. The Middle East has a poor record as far as domestic violence is concerned. Men on women violence is neither new nor confined to Arab societies. Public opinion polling in Turkey suggests that at least forty per cent of women have been the subject of battery by their male partners. Domestic violence is also a serious issue in Israeli society, a reflection in part perhaps of the stress of living in an insecure political environment.

If feminised values are regarded as tantamount to weakness within a rigidly conventional dual gender context across the region, it is obvious that other forms of sexuality from homosexuality to transgender reassignment are vilified, even in otherwise liberal circles. Yet, it is clear that preferences such as homosexuality do exist, in spite of the proud, infamous 2007 boast of the Iranian president, Mahmoud Ahmadinejad, that there are no homosexuals in Iran. If the phenomenon is largely undetectable in Iran this is presumably a reflection of self-preservation, because the practice has been outlawed and made a capital offence. Rare public demonstrations of defiance, such as a gay protest on one of the cruise ships that habitually ply the Nile, are handled roughly. Extreme stigma is associated with certain types of diseases associated with sexual transmission, notably HIV/Aids.

The Middle East is a male dominated region. This is almost as true for Christian Arab society as it is for Muslim Arab society. It is arguably more so for the ultra-Orthodox, some ten per cent of the population in Israel. The bare fact is that men – as fathers, brothers, husbands and state officials – tend to take the vast majority of decisions that affect women's lives. In general, women are seriously under-represented in places of political power. This is changing, but from a low base. Women are more visible in certain settings, such as the university campus, where they often represent a majority of students, but this does not translate into good prospects for getting a job. Women also suffer from being an arena over which ideological men argue. Man's 'women agenda' ranges from how women should dress to the conditions governing marriage and divorce to the nature of education on offer. Levels of illiteracy are stubbornly higher among females than males. By and large, wealthy, well-to-do and educated women live good lives; poorer, lower status and illiterate women endure the same miserable existence as their menfolk … only worse.

Conclusion

The Middle East has given the world tremendous cultural and intellectual gifts. This legacy needs to be understood and valued. But, having enriched the world with the three leading monotheistic religions, could it also be the site of Armageddon, the place where the world comes to an end? Consider the Islamic Republic of Iran's widely suspected desire to develop a nuclear weapons capability, Israel's presumed possession of more than sixty warheads, and the consequent combustible mix of their concurrent existence. American and European authorities certainly appear to think so, having adopted policy to try to prevent Iranian proliferation. With up to twelve other regional states having expressed an intention to acquire a nuclear capacity for civilian use (but with weaponisation beckoning) the prospect is not a comforting one. Imagine the challenge of arms control in such circumstances? For a region that claims the ancient site of the Garden of Eden (in modern day Iraq) there would be a certain symmetry to such an outcome. The cycle of humankind beginning and ending in the same place.

Yet it is hard to believe that the end would really be nigh as a consequence of developments in the Middle East, even in the event of actual Iranian–Israeli hostilities. The Israelis will enjoy a qualitative and quantitative nuclear edge over their rivals for a long time to come. Their superiority can be expected to deter any Iranian temptation to first usage. A nuclear attack or exchange is always possible, but as with the Arab–Israeli war in 1967, such an exchange would most likely be born of a miscalculation to which the region succumbs periodically. With Israel occupying a small area of territory, as in 1967 it could not allow the opposition a first strike, and especially not a nuclear one. Miscalculation is more likely than the deliberate act of a maverick local leader. Dr Strangelove, the mad scientist of the early 1960s film of the same name, remember, was not a Middle Easterner. Even under such a scenario it would be a long time before such an exchange translates into a global catastrophe. The world has more to fear from a nuclear confrontation between India and Pakistan.

For all of its global self-importance, the Middle East remains a region that fails to punch its weight on the international stage. The Arab world, the region's dominant demography and geography, and comprising most of its states, remains deeply preoccupied with itself. Like most peoples with any sense of collective self-worth the Arabs view themselves as superior to those around them, but to much less practical effect than other peoples with a mission, such as the Chinese or the Indians. The Arab world remains big on consumption but low on development.

The Arab world still fails to comprehend how the greatness of the Arab–Islamic conquest of 1400 years ago doubly dissolved, first into warring empires and then into more parochial struggles. Still less is it reconciled to what followed: 400 years of subservience (four times China's 'one hundred years of humiliation'). It is preoccupied with the period of European colonialism and the formative impact that its neighbouring region has had upon it. It has allowed the existence of the state system to restrict and constrain it, like a man wearing a suit several sizes too small for him.

This preoccupation with the past makes it difficult for the Middle East to transcend its relatively recent political experience. It dreams of a new greatness, but without producing any strategy for its realisation, nuclearisation apart. Rather than embrace the states of the region as an irreversible reality or overturn them as an undesired anachronism it has done neither.

It has complained of its lack of ownership of the creation of the region's states but without taking effective action to change the political landscape. Instead, it has allowed itself to become disempowered by its past. This helps to explain the region's fondness for conspiracy theories, alibis for an absence of decisive action, and the still commonly expressed view that just about every foreigner in their midst is a spy. The outcome has been a victim culture, whereby the region's self-image is of a largely passive collection of players, prey to the manipulations of unscrupulous outsiders.

There have been moments when the Arab world seemed as if it might be able to move on. The leadership of Nasser and the invigorating movement of Arab nationalism offered redemption, but the project ran aground in the face of the divisions of the Arab states. The oil income of the 1970s and early 1980s promised a new start. Great wealth seemed poised to deliver development for the region and liberation from the dependent periphery of the capitalist world. Yet oil wealth brought its own distortions. It provided little other than shiny trinkets and spasmodic consumption splurges.

More recently, Islam, not in its spiritual or mystical form, but as a political philosophy has been offered as the latest source of salvation, not merely for the Arabs but for the whole region. The corrupt and self-serving nature of the region's two incumbent Islamist regimes, the Islamic Republic in Iran, and the cruel and repressive regime in Sudan, have not as yet discredited this notion. Far from it. In an illustration of the paucity of new ideas in the region Islamism remains the only alternative political project on offer, from Morocco in the west, through Egypt, Jordan and Syria, to Saudi Arabia in the east. Incumbent regimes have hung on hitherto, in the face of such pressures, the latest chapter in a political authoritarianism that has marked the region for a thousand years. But there is no guarantee that this will continue to be the case.

The non-Arab nation-states of Iran, Israel and Turkey, meanwhile, are the outsider entities of the Middle East, perennially out of place compared to the ethnic and confessional homogeneity of most of their Arab neighbours. They have no community of states beyond the Middle East with which naturally to bond. Turkey has sought to ameliorate this through its sputtering relationship with the EU, to date with only brittle success. All three remain cursed to live within a region over which they can never exercise real ownership; which at best tolerates them, is frequently suspicious of them and which at times tries to undermine them. Little wonder then that the main fault-lines of conflict in the region have comprised Iran, Israel or Turkey and some combination of the rest.

There are, for sure, potentially mould-breaking forces. These include new media literate young people, entrepreneurial businessmen, medical researchers, artists and high achieving academics. The trouble is that most of these Middle Easterners have had to defect to or been born or brought up in the West in order to unleash their full creative imaginations. They do have some counterparts in the region, but they remain confined to the edges of Middle Eastern societies, and are stifled by oppressively conservative ideas and repressive regime enforcers. As such, they are ill-equipped to challenge the prevailing power structures, whether of regime dominated clans or the prevalent conservative orthodoxies of religion. They are weighed down by the expectations of a deference society, and are unaware of how to do things any other way.

The sad fact is that beyond the Middle East's natural beauty, its rich historical legacy, the warm hospitality of its people and its array of cultural traditions, global contemporary interest in the region is dominated by negatives, of which nuclear proliferation is merely the latest and most dangerous. For many outsiders, the region is reducible to the ugly violence of the Israeli–Palestinian tragedy. Illiberalism, most notoriously in the form of human rights abuses, is still rife. Lurching oil prices threaten to exacerbate world economic depression. Many find it difficult to get beyond the Middle East as the source of inspiration, brains and foot soldiers for a section of international terrorism, even to the magnitude of a 9/11. Again, many see it as contributing towards the creation of the conditions for a 'clash of civilisations', especially one based on so-called religious values and their associated cultural practices. The image problem from which the Middle East suffers, and which was mentioned at the outset of this volume, looks like enduring for a long time to come.

Further reading

History

The authoritative history of the region has for some time been William L. Cleveland, *A History of the Modern Middle East* 3rd ed. (Westview, 2004). Its main competitors are: James Gelvin, *The Modern Middle East: A History* (Oxford University Press, 2005); Arthur Goldschmidt, *A Concise History of the Middle East* 8th ed. (Westview, 2006); M.E.Yapp, *The Near East Since the First World War: A History to 1995* (Longman, 1996). The best overview exclusively of the Arabs is still Albert Hourani, *A History of the Arab Peoples* (Faber & Faber, 1991). A handful of thematic textbooks exist on the region, notably James A. Bill & Robert Springborg, *Politics in the Middle East* (Glenview, 1991), Roger Owen, *State, Power & Politics in the Modern East* (Routledge, 1992) and Beverly Milton-Edwards, *Contemporary Politics in the Middle East* (Polity Press, 2000). For excellent histories of individual Middle Eastern countries, see the current Cambridge University Press series, which has so far seen the publication of volumes on: Egypt, Iraq, Jordan, Modern Palestine, Saudi Arabia, Tunisia and Yemen.

Conflict

For the standard work on the Middle East and international relations, coverage including the most recent US-led invasion of Iraq, see Louise Fawcett ed., *International Relations of the Middle East* 2nd ed. (Oxford University Press, 2009). For an important treatment of individual states within the overall region, see Ray Hinnebusch and Anoush Ehteshami, *The Foreign Policies of Middle East States* (Rienner, 2002). For a comprehensive history of the Arab/Palestinian–Israel dispute, see Charles D. Smith, *Palestine and the Arab-Israeli Conflict* (St. Martin's Press, 1992). A favourite work on the 1967 war is *The Politics of Miscalculation in the Middle East* by Richard B. Parker (Indiana UP, 1993). For the struggle between Israel and the Arabs, see Avi Shlaim, *The Iron Wall. Israel and the Arab World* (Penguin, 2001). For the most extensive coverage of the first Gulf war in one book, see Lawrence Friedman & Efraim Karsh, *The Gulf Conflict, 1990/91* (Princeton University Press, 2003).

Development

For the best region-wide book on political economy, see Alan Richards and John Waterbury, *A Political Economy of the Middle East. State, Class and Economic Development* 3rd ed. (Westview, 1996). For a general economic history, see Roger Owen and Sevket Pamuk, *A History of Middle East Economies in the Twentieth Century* (Tauris, 1998). Clement Henry and Robert Springborg, *Globalisation and the Politics of Development in the Middle East* (Cambridge UP, 2001) is now the standard work on globalisation and the region. For the key works on the rentier state see the respective chapters by Giacomo Luciani and Hazem Beblawi in Luciani ed., *The Arab State* (Routledge, 1990).

Governance

For an enduring classic analysing Arab political elites, see Michael Hudson, *Arab Politics. The Search for Legitimacy* (Yale University Press, 1977). For the towering work on the modern

Arab state see Nazih Ayubi, *Over-stating the Arab State* (Tauris, 1995). The leading volume on democratisation and its absence in the region is still Ghassan Salame, ed., *Democracy Without Democrats. The Renewal of Politics in the Muslim World* (Tauris, 1995). For books concentrating on the conservative regimes, see Michael Herb, *All in the Family: Absolutism, Revolution and Democracy in the Middle Eastern Monarchies* (State University of New York Press, 1999); Joseph Kostiner, ed., *Middle East Monarchies: The Challenge of Modernity* (Lynne Rienner, 2000). With so many works concentrating on why there is little change, see Robert Satloff, ed., *The Politics of Change in the Middle East* (Westview, 1993) as an antidote.

Leadership

There are surprisingly no comparative, thematic works on leadership in the Middle East. The nearest one gets is an enduring classic: Majid Khadduri, *Arab Contemporaries. The Role of Personalities in Politics* (Johns Hopkins Press, 1973). There are, however, a number of very good biographies. For the pick in terms of giving insight into their subjects, see: Nigel Ashton, *King Hussein of Jordan. A Political Life* (Yale UP, 2008); Derek Hopwood, *Habib Bourgeiba of Tunisia* (MacMillan, 1992); Andrew Mango, *Ataturk* (John Murray, 2004); Baqer Moin, *Khomeini, The Life of the Ayatollah* (Tauris, 1997); and Patrick Seale, *Asad of Syria. The Struggle for the Middle East* (Tauris, 1988).

Society

On the very important issue of kin politics, see Philip Khoury, and Joseph Kostiner, ed., *Tribes and State Formation in the Middle*

East (Tauris, London, 1992). Popular culture and youth issues in general are not well served in the published literature. For three exceptions see: Ali Akbar Mahdi ed., *Teen Life in the Middle East* (Greenwood Press, 2003); Andrew Hammond, *Pop Culture Arab World! Media, Arts and Lifestyle* (ABC Clio, 2005); Walter Armbrust, *Mass Mediations: New Approaches to Popular Culture in the Middle East and Beyond* (Univ. of California Press, 2000). For a recent title on media in the region, see Naomi Sakr, *Arab Media and Political Renewal: Community, Legitimacy and Public Life* (Tauris, 2007).

Religion

For the best single work on Islam and politics see Dale Eichelman, ' and James Piscatori, *Muslim Politics* (Princeton University Press, 1996). Three contemporary classics on the issue of political Islam are: Nazih Ayubi, *Political Islam* (Routledge, 1991); John Esposito and John Voll, *Islam and Democracy* (Oxford University Press, 1996); and, more controversially, Olivier Roy, *The Failure of Political Islam* (Tauris, 1994). For the best introduction to the Islamic revolution in Iran see Nikki Keddie, *Modern Iran. Roots and Results of Revolution* (Yale University Press, 2006). For attempts to make sense of religion and politics post 9/11, see Bernard Lewis, *What Went Wrong? The Clash between Islam and Modernity in the Middle East* (Harper Perennial, 2002).

Gender

Feisty and idiosyncratic, Fatima Mernissi, *Beyond the Veil* (John Wiley & Sons, 1975) was the breakthrough book on women written from the region. Leila Ahmed ed., *Women in Islam* (Yale University Press, 1992) is the work of reference. Laurie Brand, *Women, the State and Political Liberalisation: Middle East and North African Experiences* (Columbia University Press, 1998) gives more of a political studies perspective. Deniz Kandiyoti, ed., *Gendering the Middle East* (Tauris, 1996) approaches the issue from a critical theory perspective.

Index